Florida

- A (☛ in the text denotes a highly recommended sight
- A complete A–Z of practical information starts on p.101
- Extensive mapping on cover flaps and throughout the text.

Berlitz Publishing Company, Inc.

Princeton   **Mexico City**   **Dublin**   **Eschborn**   **Singapore**

Text: Martin Gostelow
Editors: Tanya Colbourne
Photography: Jacques Bétant, Aram Gesar, Martin Gostelow
Layout: Media Content Marketing, Inc.
Cartography: 🔵 Falk - Verlag, Munich

Thanks to British airways, Lee County Visitor and Convention Bureau, Greater Miami Convention and Visitors Bureau, Naples Area Chamber of Commerce, Spaceport USA, Universal Studios Florida, and Walt Disney World Co, for their invaluable help in the preparation of this guide.

Although the publisher tries to insure the accuracy of all the information in this book, changes are inevitable and errors may result. The publisher cannot be responsible for any resulting loss, inconvenience, or injury. If you find an error in this guide, please let the editors know by writing to Berlitz Publishing Company, 400 Alexander Park, Princeton, NJ 08540-6306.

ISBN 2-8315-6301-1
Revised 1998 – Fourth Printing April 1999

Printed in Switzerland by Weber SA, Bienne
049/904 RP

CONTENTS

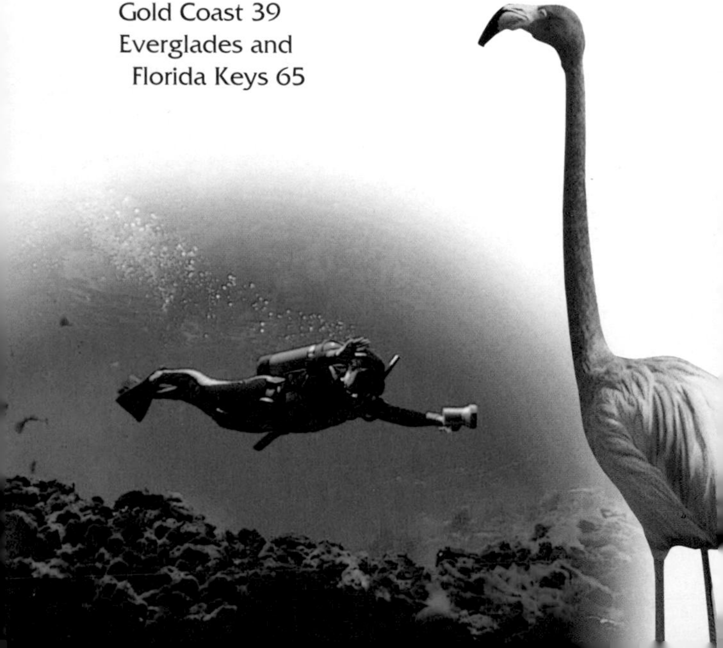

FLORIDA

FLORIDA AND THE FLORIDIANS

The southeast corner of the United States juts so far south it almost reaches the tropics. Almost 640 km (400 miles) long and roughly 200 km (130 miles) wide, this sun-drenched peninsula is so fringed by offshore islands that its total coastline is practically trebled. The climate has enticed everyone — from multi-millionaires to pensioners on a tight budget; sports stars to student "spring-breakers"; and refugees fleeing the winters of the northern United States.

Florida matches California as a pacesetter in new ideas about fashion and entertainment, and Floridians enjoy a lifestyle only made possible by the generous gifts of nature. Film makers, high-technology enterprises, and new businesses have all been persuaded to settle here. Even Mickey Mouse has taken up residence! And the Sunshine State has gone international, drawing the most unlikely combination of immigrants and tourists — a mosaic of sun-starved European holiday-makers, South American moguls, and immigrants from the islands of the Caribbean.

Florida reinvents itself with every generation, from steaming swamp to tourist magnet to den of corruption, from retirement home to space base and back again to holiday paradise. Each time, something of the previous incarnation remains. The result is a kind of schizophrenia — Florida doesn't know whether to be sleepy and sub-tropical or fast and trendy. You'll be jolted constantly by the contrasts. Great wealth is juxtaposed with dire poverty; concrete sprawl adjoins impenetrable jungle; fine art stands hand-in-hand with kitsch; beaches throng with the obese and the svelte. Even the traffic seems to reflect this dichotomy — dreamers in cruise control versus the daredevil exhibitionists on the Miami freeways.

Florida's magnificent beaches —
idyllic playground for children and adults alike.

The most southerly of the continental states (only Hawaii is closer to the equator), Florida endures scorching summers when you'll be greeted by a blast of heat and humidity. The reward comes in the form of mild winters when locals and visitors smugly read about fog and snow dislocating the cities of the north, while Miami basks in the nation's highest temperatures and the citrus crop ripens on the trees.

Topographically Florida is more subtle in its appeal, a flat plain with the highest point a mere 105 metres (345 feet) above sea level. The coastline, longer than any state's save Alaska, is wonderfully varied. A chain of offshore islands shields the Intra-Coastal Waterway. All along the coast, pelicans patrol above the waves, occasionally plummeting in a crash-dive when they spot a fish. Giant turtles can be seen wading ashore, while exquisite shells roll in the surf.

Along the Gulf Coast sweep miles of palm-fringed white sandy beaches, whose shallow waters provide safe bathing for children. The Atlantic beaches are more golden, with the chance of bigger waves appealing to surfers. The water is warm thanks to the Gulf Stream, making it a paradise for anyone who loves water recreation.

Inland, grassy plains shimmer with an estimated 30,000 lakes. The landscape is divided by cattle ranches, fragrant orange groves, pine and cypress forests, and homely small towns. Exotic flowers are not restricted to the many lush botanical gardens. In this climate anyone can grow them. From the lakes, the overflow of warm water seeps south and west through hundreds of square miles of grassland, culminating in the mangrove swamps of the Everglades — pride of southern Florida. Here you can sail, canoe, fish, or explore the trails in search of alligators, southern bald eagles, or (probably in vain) the elusive Florida panther.

A holiday in Florida provides every opportunity to try your hand at a host of outdoor sports. Waterskiing, scuba-diving, surfing, tennis, golf, or riding — whatever appeals to you, you may be sure friendly and professional instructors will be close at hand with advice. Many resorts feature video-equipped tennis and golf clinics with computer analysis of your faults. All types of spa facilities abound, offering exercise programmes, massages, and bubbling jacuzzis.

Whatever your preference — be it exploring the mangrove swamps, visiting the Kennedy Space Center, or even admiring the world's largest collection of seashells — you'll be overwhelmed by the choice of things to see and do. Soon you'll become blasé about the "World's Biggest and Best" labels.

For most holiday-makers, eating is an important element in their enjoyment. Dining in Florida is informal and an indulgence undertaken with great gusto. Portions tend to be enormous and the famous "all-you-can-eat" buffets provide a daunting challenge even to the most ardent gourmand. Eating and drinking goes on unabated at all times of the day and night. The variety is endless — choose stone crabs or a live lobster from a tank, go out to a traditional barbecue, or venture into one of Miami's superb Cuban restaurants in Little Havana for something really special.

Florida's appeal is immediate. More than that, it grows on you. For the thousands who flock to the Sunshine State, exchanging overcoats and business suits for cut-off shorts and sports gear, there is the feeling that this is the place to be. Daiquiris in hand, the local Floridians will laugh and say they know the feeling well — it's called "getting sand in your shoes."

Peddle power in
Coconut Grove.

The Ethnic Mix

Florida's kinship with the American Deep South can be felt most in the north of the state, around Tallahassee and Jacksonville — an Anglo-Saxon and African-American population, largely. But from the time of its Spanish discovery, the state has always had a pronounced Latin flavour. Cuba is only 90 miles (145 km) from Key West, a fact which has often affected Florida's history and still does. Cuban exiles make up the largest contingent in Miami, lending great colour to the street life, spice to the cuisine, and an edge to the politics. Even second-generation Cubans are fiercely loyal to a certain image of the "old country," and vociferous about past and current events there. The Latin presence was further augmented by an influx of Nicaraguans during their homeland's troubles. And more recently still, there has been an increasing number of Caribbean immigrants, particularly from Haiti.

Florida is a magnet, too, for the New Yorker. Accents in the supermarkets and around the swimming pools of Miami Beach and the Gold Coast are more likely to be laced with the heavy ironies of Brooklyn and Queens than the good-ol'-boy cheerfulness of the neighbouring southern states of Georgia and Alabama. Italians, Greeks, Scandinavians running cruise lines, Brits hungry for sunshine — think of a national group and you'll find them here.

The Florida Keys have always attracted a cosmopolitan mixture of bohemians — artists, writers, and seekers after the good life flock here from all over America and beyond. This lively bunch of eccentrics defy any ethnic classification at all.

Key West does have its own proud "Conchs" (named after the shellfish). They trace their ancestry back to the American Revolution, when loyalists to the British crown fled first to the Bahamas and then on to the Keys, where their community still runs the fishing business and keeps aloof from "interlopers."

A BRIEF HISTORY

The flat landscape of Florida emerged long ago from the sea, augmented by silt washed down by the mighty rivers of the north and coral reefs growing in the warm waters. In prehistoric times sabre-toothed tigers prowled through the wetlands. Woolly mammoths, giant bison, and even camels roamed the plains.

The first human beings arrived about 15,000 years ago, perhaps from farther north, but possibly from Central America. They lived by hunting and fishing and especially from the generous supplies of shellfish. In south and central Florida, in fact, some of the highest hills are the oyster shell mounds piled up by these earliest inhabitants. Some mounds can still be seen, although many disappeared in modern times when the material in them was used to make roads and tracks through the swamps.

Facts and Figures

Population: 9,000,000.

Geography: 151,670 km (58,560 sq. miles) in area with the second-longest coastline of any U.S. state (1,350 miles/2,170 km).

State Capital: Tallahassee (population 90,000).

Climate: Semi-tropical in the southern half of the state, less extreme in northern areas; sunshine can be relied upon most of the year; humidity may be very high in summer. Chance of hurricanes from June to November.

Economy: Tourism and service industries, citrus fruit, and vegetable growing, cattle-raising, tobacco, food processing, chemicals, electrical and transportation equipment, space technology.

Getting there: Jet flight from New York 2½ hours, London 9 hours.

By the standards of the times, the early Floridians had an easier life than most hunter-gatherers. Judging by surviving pieces, they had time to create artworks such as shell jewellery and beautiful statuettes. Ceremonial burials also suggest an organized religious life. Around 1450 B.C., they found that despite the low-fertility soil, the climate made it possible to cultivate crops such as maize, squash, cassava, and peppers. Archaeologists have recently dated systems of drainage canals to that period.

On the eve of the European discovery of the New World, Florida's indigenous population numbered some tens of thousands, divided into five nations. Chief of these were the Timucua of the north, the Apalachee in the Panhandle, and the Calusa in the southwest.

European Discovery

Columbus was not far from Florida when he bumped into the island of Hispaniola (now Haiti and the Dominican Republic) on his way to "the Indies" in 1492. Other early explorers may have searched the Florida coast for a passage to the Pacific, but credit for the discovery of the land goes to Juan Ponce de León (1460–1521). Bored with life in Spain after the Moorish wars ended, he set out with Columbus on his second expedition in 1493. The voyage rekindled his taste for adventure, and by 1508 Ponce was on his way to Puerto Rico. He became the island's governor, but soon lost his position to the more influential Diego Columbus, son of the navigator.

In 1512, the Spanish king commissioned Ponce de León to find and explore the fabled "Isle of Bimini." The island, so legend said, concealed a spring with the miraculous power to restore youth to the aged. No doubt Ponce, 52 years old at the time, was inspired with hope. If it didn't work, there was still the prospect of gold and slave labour to provide for his old age.

Setting sail for the Bahamas in search of Bimini, Ponce landed instead on the Florida coast, on 2 April 1513. He named the new country after the date in his calendar, *Pascua Florida*, the Feast of Flowers at Easter. From his first land-fall, near present-day St. Augustine, Ponce and his crew sailed down the coast, past Cape Canaveral, along the Florida Keys, and out to the Dry Tortugas. From there they continued north along the Gulf Coast to Charlotte Harbor before returning to Puerto Rico after an eight-month voyage. Ponce had missed Bimini, but he had found an immense land full of promise, which his grateful sovereign granted him the right to conquer, govern, and colonize.

Blighted Hopes

Ponce's discovery was to prove a bitter disappointment to him. On a second voyage to Florida in 1521, the explorer took along two ships, 200 colonists, livestock, and farm implements. Though Ponce knew from his first visit that the Calusa Indians at Charlotte Harbor were hostile, he chose to land there nevertheless. His party were in the process of building shelters when fierce warriors attacked. Ponce himself was badly wounded by an arrow, and was carried back to his ship. By the time the disillusioned settlers reached Cuba their leader was near death. He was buried in Puerto Rico.

The pattern of great expectations and dashed hopes was to repeat itself in later ventures. Pánfilo de Narváez, a follower of Cortés, set out from Cuba in 1528 with 600 soldiers and colonists, but quickly lost 200 of his party in skirmishes. Marching inland from Tampa Bay, they expected to find food and water easily, but in the event they almost starved. The fabled gold was nowhere to be found; the only inhabitants were poor Indian women and children living in mud huts. Panic-stricken in a strange and hostile land, Narváez and his followers built makeshift boats and set sail for Mexico, which they thought was nearby. Of the 242 who manned the boats, only four ever reached Mexico City. Narváez was not among them. A search party sent out by Narváez's wife also disappeared.

Pedro Menénez de Avilés, founder of St. Augustine.

Yet another ill-fated expedition was led by Hernando de Soto. Already rich and famous at the age of 36, the Spanish explorer left Cuba for Florida in 1538 with 600 optimistic volunteers. When they landed in Tampa Bay on 30 May 1539, they were met by Juan Ortiz, a survivor from the search party sent to find Narváez. Ortiz could now speak the Indian languages, and was to prove invaluable as a guide and interpreter. But this auspicious beginning was not followed by similar good fortune. Though de Soto's band marched as far as Oklahoma and Kansas in search of riches, they found none. The farther they went, the more determined they became to continue until they discovered something, but they never did. Half of the men, including de Soto himself, died during the four-year odyssey. The survivors made their way back to Cuba empty-handed.

The First Permanent Settlement

Control of Florida's east coast became strategically important as soon as Spanish treasure fleets began to sail along it, following the Gulf Stream. News that France was taking an interest at last drove Spain to found a durable colony. On 8 September 1565, Pedro Menéndez de Avilés and a detachment of soldiers arrived at the mouth of the St. John's river near present-day Jacksonville, where a party of French Huguenots had been struggling along in their small settlement at Fort Caroline.

At this time the two great European nations were engaged in a bitter contest for colonial domination, and a battle was certain. The French were caught by surprise, with their ships away at sea, and were easily overcome. Later, the French fleet was wrecked on the coast in a storm, and the Spanish were able to round up the survivors. Faced with the problem of what to do with the captives, Menéndez decided that the threat to his own party, with its limited food supply, was too great to ignore. Sparing women and children, Catholics and musicians, he put the rest to the sword "not as Frenchmen, but as Lutherans."

About 48 km (30 miles) south of Fort Caroline, Menéndez founded the first permanent settlement in North America, the colony of St. Augustine. It suffered from sporadic Indian attacks and in 1586 was raided by the English privateer Sir Francis Drake. The difficulties of defending the outpost were plain, but it was judged essential, and in response to later English, Indian, and pirate assaults, the Spanish constructed a massive fortress of stone which still stands today.

Step back in time into this St Augustine home erected by North America's first permanent settlers.

Castillo de San Narcos, a 17th-century Spanish fortress in St. Augustine.

Imperial Rivals

In 1682 Robert Cavelier Sieur de La Salle completed his long journey down the Mississippi, claiming the entire river valley for the King of France, Louis XIV. When Louis attempted to seat his grandson on the throne of Spain, England was quick to see the peril. Spain and France united could dictate to the rest of Europe and the world.

The War of the Spanish Succession in 1702 brought English forces deep into Florida. Though the fortress at St. Augustine survived an eight-week siege and never fell, the English wiped out most of Spain's other military outposts and religious missions in four years of war.

With Spanish power in decline, England and France could concentrate on fighting each other for domination of North America. The Seven Years' War in Europe spread to the New

World as the "French and Indian War." Despite Indian support, French forces went down in defeat, leaving the English were defeated masters of the continent. In 1763 Florida was officially ceded to England.

With the new European overlords came another shift in population. Descendants of the original American Indians, shattered by European diseases, the slave trade, and internal feuds, left Florida with the Spanish to find more peaceful homes in the West and in Cuba. Their farms and villages were taken over by a mixture of tribes from Alabama and Georgia called the Seminoles (from the Spanish *cimarrones*, "runaway" or "wild").

The Seminoles were courted by English traders bearing pots, knives, guns, and axes. The government gave grants to organize plantations, and soon indigo, rice, turpentine, sugar, and oranges became lucrative exports. The English had found a way to make money where the Spanish had failed to find gold.

Lost Colony

After the British defeat in the American War of Independence, Florida was returned to Spanish rule by the Treaty of Paris of 1783. But the allegiance of Florida's Seminole and European inhabitants remained with Britain, which had done so much to develop the land. In a further bizarre turn of events, the British,

An 18th-century cannon.

now allied with Spain in the Napoleonic wars, landed forces in western Florida in 1814, only to withdraw again when U.S. troops, under the future president Andrew Jackson, marched into the disputed territory. Further American incursions marked this final unhappy spell of Spanish rule. Unable to control Florida, Spain ceded it to the United States in 1819. Jackson became its first U.S. governor in 1821.

American settlers flooded into Florida, causing consternation among the long-time inhabitants. The Seminoles were gradually pushed off the fertile lands of the north and into the Everglades. Then, in 1830, Andrew Jackson, now president, signed an act of Congress ordering all American Indians to move to new lands in the frontier territories to the west. Some accepted; others stood and fought. In the Seminole War of 1835–1842 it became clear that conventional U.S. forces were unsuited to combating the hit-and-run tactics of opponents who could disappear into the steaming swamps of southern Florida. The Seminole leader Osceola

Whitehall, the Palm Beach mansion of railway baron Henry Flagler.

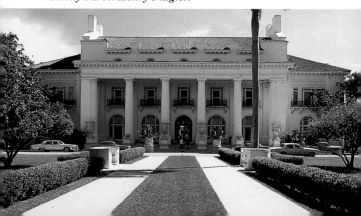

was seized, although under a flag of truce, and died in prison not long after. His followers did not give up the struggle but were forced deeper into the Everglades. The war ended at last in stalemate, but only a few hundred Seminoles remained, in scattered villages.

Civil War

With peace came growing prosperity, and, in 1845, statehood for Florida as the 27th member of the Union. There was a new wave of northern immigrants, but for the most part local power rested on plantation owners, who depended on slave labour. Thus Florida took the side of the southern states in the American Civil War, seceding from the Union in 1861 and joining the Confederacy. But in a replay of the Spanish-English conflict, Union forces from the north easily captured and occupied most of Florida's ports and forts. Many Confederate troops were sent to fight distant battles, and those that remained were mainly engaged in raiding supply lines.

With the war's end in 1865 came nominal freedom for the slaves, although many in fact continued to work for their former masters in scarcely better conditions. Their hopes for equal rights were dashed and Florida acquired a corrupt, segregationist state government. However, the war and its aftermath had brought the state to the attention of northern investors. It had suffered less destruction than the rest of the South and was to develop quite differently.

Railroad Barons and Early Tourists

By the last quarter of the 19th century, a number of enterprising businessmen had seen the potential of the state's geography and climate. Two names stand out: Henry Morrison Flagler and Henry Bradley Plant. Both possessed the kind of pioneering spirit that was the driving force of that expansionary era. What was more, they had the money to turn their dreams into reality. Flagler's East Coast Railroad drove through swamp and jungle, reaching Miami in 1896 and eventually spanning the water to Key West. Henry Plant's lines to Tampa and beyond opened up central and western Florida.

It didn't take long for the good news to spread, and soon tourists were descending in droves. Permanent settlers came, too: between 1870 and 1890, Florida's population doubled, and it has continued to grow ever since. So has the pressure on land. It was the memorably named state governor, Napoleon Bonaparte Broward, who dug the first spadeful of earth in 1905 to begin a massive drainage programme. Hundreds of miles of canals and dikes converted huge tracts of the Everglades into dry land. Hailed at the time, the effort is now looked upon as a disaster by conservationists, and limited attempts are being made to reverse the process in places.

The tourist boom became a near riot in the mid-1920s, when real estate prices began to soar. Suddenly, thousands of Americans wanted to own a piece of Florida for vacations, retirement, or just as an investment. Over 2,000 arrivals a day flooded into the state, and soon the railroads forbade any railcar to advertise Miami as its destination. Then reality began to redress the balance. A ship from up north carrying would-be Floridians sank in Biscayne Bay; a hurricane in 1926 wrought havoc in the Miami area; the bottom fell out of land prices, and with the onset of the Great Depression in 1929 the bonanza was over.

World War II and After

Florida's economy didn't really recover until the beginning of World War II, when thousands of recruits arrived to be trained at the state's bases. These modern soldiers and sailors fell under the same spell as others before them. When peace came, many remembering the warmth of the southern sun, returned to Florida to start businesses, raise families, and later, to retire. The state's economy was diversified. Agriculture was expanded to provide winter vegetables for the north and more fruit, especially citrus. Cattle farmers

---

Hurricane Who?

Alice or Arthur? It used to be traditional to give women's names to hurricanes: now, to avoid sexism, they are alternated. But whatever people call them makes no difference to these frighteningly powerful tropical storms which sweep through Florida from time to time with winds of up to 240 km (150 miles) an hour. The raging gales, torrents of rain, and flood tides may sound exciting to an outsider but, in fact, they're terrifying and often tragic.

The worst hurricane to hit Florida in 60 years took place on 24 August 1992. The strongest storm in 60 years, Hurricane Andrew struck Florida near the small town of Homestead, 48 km (30 miles) south of Miami Beach, then swept across the state and into the Gulf of Mexico. Twenty-seven people were killed and hundreds of millions of dollars' worth of damage was caused. Fortunately, most of the devastation was confined to a relatively small area in the southern part of Dade County. Massive relief efforts, including a huge "Labor of Love" project organized on America's Labor Day weekend, meant that virtually all of Florida's hotels and attractions were up and running within a few days of the hurricane.

Statistically, hurricanes hit Florida only once every seven years, between the months of June and November. Your chance of being in the wrong place at the wrong time is therefore minimal.

---

profited from cheap land prices in Florida's interior. The 1959 revolution in Cuba brought an influx of 300,000 Cubans, swelling Miami's population.

Recent decades have seen the love affair with Florida continue. Jumbo jets bring vacationers in greater numbers than ever. Winter sun-seekers drive down the interstate highways from frigid northern cities in just a couple of days.

Travel has yet another dimension in Florida: it was from Cape Canaveral on the Atlantic coast that America first probed into space. Beginning in 1950 with the launch of a modified German V-2, the Cape has seen the blast-off of ever more powerful rockets. From Kennedy Space Center, American astronauts set out to make man's first landing on the moon in 1969. Today, crowds flock to "Space Coast" to watch the space shuttles lift off into orbit.

Changing Patterns

When Walt Disney quietly started to buy up land near Orlando in the late 1960s, he began a process that was to alter Florida tourism beyond recognition. There had long been a handful of purpose-built holiday "attractions," but when Walt Disney World opened in 1971 it made them look amateur and insignificant. Some rose to the challenge, some went under. Now, Disney World has four times the facilities it opened with and is the most popular vacation destination on earth. Other theme parks cluster around it to get some of the action, and Orlando has turned from a sleepy market town to the city with more hotel rooms than any other in the United States.

European travellers find Miami and Orlando among the New World's most accessible cities. Refugees from the cold north and the Caribbean still arrive in the thousands. The Spanish explorers sought gold and the fountain of youth. The objectives of today's visitors are not so different.

WHERE TO GO

In terms of size, Florida ranks only 22nd among American states, but at more than 58,000 square miles (150,000 sq. km) it's the size of England and Wales combined. There's more than enough to see and do to keep you going for months, let alone the average two-week holiday. So you will have to make choices. The Gulf Coast or the Atlantic Coast? Combined with Walt Disney World? Miami and southern Florida as well? Or instead?

Most visitors hire a car. It's undoubtly the best means of getting around, even if you plan to stay in one area. Rates are economical, fuel is cheap, the roads are good and not too crowded, and it's easy to find your way.

In this book we travel north from Miami up the Atlantic Coast through Fort Lauderdale, Palm Beach, and the "Space Coast" to St. Augustine. Then we look at booming Orlando and Central Florida, home of Walt Disney World and several more theme parks, before going south to the Everglades and the Florida Keys. Finally, we visit the fast-expanding resorts of the Gulf Coast, travelling north from Naples to Clearwater Beach. But first comes a famous American vacation spot, which has recently undergone an exciting revival.

MIAMI BEACH

The city of Miami Beach, "where the sun spends the winter," is in fact a narrow 11-km (7-mile) strip of land separated from mainland Miami by Biscayne Bay and connected to it by causeways. It's here that you'll find something of the opulence and brash taste that have become as much a part of the American legend as the Wild West.

Collins Avenue, the north-south spine of the island, is lined by hotels and holiday apartments. The resort's heyday was in the 1950s, when vast pleasure palaces aspired to be the biggest and most luxurious, 20 years later it was no longer fashionable here. Now the place has picked itself up and is being discovered by a new generation. Hotels have had face-lifts, and still try to outdo each other, but except in high season the competition mainly takes the form of offering special rates.

In contrast are the more modest Art-Deco hotels and self-service apartments of **South Beach**, an area developed in the 1930s and now revitalized. The seafront along **Ocean Drive** benefits from a wide strip of grass, and, especially between about 10th and 13th streets, it has become a trendy place to be seen. Real or would-be models and other "beautiful people" parade at the open-air bars, while bikers and roller skaters cut in and out of the sunset traffic snarl.

The **Bass Museum of Art** (just off Collins Avenue at 21st Street) has a small but select collection including Baroque

The world-famous resort of Miami Beach,
where the sun spends the winter.

sculpture, Regency portraits, Tibetan and Nepalese bronzes, and, appropriately, architectural designs of the 1930s.

The Miami Beach business district, just north of South Beach, includes Lincoln Road Mall, a pedestrian shopping street. Most of the modestly priced accommodations lie between South Beach and 41st Street. Then, above Arthur Godfrey Boulevard, come the top-of-the-line hotels, including the legendary **Fontainebleau Hilton**. (If you're driving north up Collins Avenue, you'll see a huge mural of the hotel apparently blocking the way.) The "Fount'n-Blue," as it's usually pronounced, is a resort in itself, with pools, water-falls, grottoes, hidden bars, shops, a tennis centre, and an aquarium. It has been modernized, but the memory lingers on of an America now found only on film, when Hollywood stars stayed regularly at the Fontainebleau.

The rambling Miami Beach **boardwalk** begins at 21st Street and runs between the big hotels and the beach as far as 46th Street. When it opened in 1984, the wooden walkway made a hit with its covered pavilions providing shaded places to sit. The beach is wide and flat but not especially at-tractive, and, is difficult to reach in places. (Too often in the United States, although the shore itself is mostly open to the public, private property bars the way and there are few points of access.) Around 74th Street you'll again find more modest hotels and a small-town feeling.

North of Miami Beach

Leading north from Miami Beach along the string of off-shore islands, Route A1A winds through the pleasant resort of **Surfside** (at about 93rd Street) and then on to **Bal Harbour**, with its waffle-faced condominiums and elegant ho-tels. Don't miss Bal Harbour Shops, a luxury mall renowned as much for its setting as for its merchandise.

Boats moored at Bal Harbour north of Miami Beach.

Farther along A1A, **Haulover Park** is sandwiched between the bay and the ocean. On the bay side, Haulover Marina has berths for dozens of fishing boats, and is the starting point for cruises along the Intra-Coastal Waterway to Fort Lauderdale. The ocean side of the park has an acceptable family beach with picnic places.

The Sunny Isles (around 167th Street) attract package-tour vacationers. You can fish from the pier, dance in the nightclubs, and see a cabaret. Close by on the mainland, just off 167th Street near U.S. 1, you'll come to the tranquil **St. Bernard's** (or the **Old Spanish) Monastery**, billed as "the oldest building in North America." In fact, it has only stood here since the 1950s! The 12th-century cloisters originally in Segovia, Spain, were bought by the press magnate William Randolph Hearst for his estate at San Simeon in California, dismantled, and shipped over in 1925. The crates were all numbered, but customs inspectors broke them open and mixed up the stones. Hearst lost interest and it was left to others to reassemble the puzzle.

Around 196th Street, **Aventura** is famous for its exclusive golf and tennis resorts, and for a shopping mall which is vast even by local standards. The resorts continue in an unbroken line to the north, but at this point we turn back to Florida's sprawling metropolis.

MIAMI

As much a Latin American as a North American city, with as many Spanish-speakers as English, Miami is a fast-moving picture. It was only a village when the railroad baron Henry Flagler was persuaded to extend his tracks this far south in 1896. Now the metropolitan population is close to 2 million and the suburbs

The Art Deco District

Thanks to the extraordinary number of buildings in the "streamlined modern" style, 2.6 sq. km (one square mile) of Miami Beach known as the **Art Deco District** has been declared a national preservation zone. Nowhere else in America is there such a concentration of architecture from the 1930s and early forties. Hotels and apartments were built at modest cost using cast concrete and stucco, decorated with chrome, stainless steel, glass blocks, and plastics. Thumbing its nose at the Depression, the flashy style set out to attract a new generation of middle-class tourists. The Miami Design Preservation League organizes guided tours of this unique quarter (tel. 672-2014). If you walk it on your own, stroll along Ocean Drive between 5th and 15th streets and the neighbouring blocks to the west.

stretch for 50 km (30 miles). Some neighbourhoods are on their way up, others are run-down, and some are definitely "no-go" areas.

The Metrorail elevated railway brings people from the northern and southern suburbs into the city centre, while the automated Metromover makes a loop round the downtown district. A ride on this one is primarily for fun and the views: the system doesn't actually cover much ground. It was built as part of a renewal programme for downtown Miami, which is certainly livelier than it was in the 1970s, although the shops are mostly of the fast-buck variety.

Flagler Street, the main east-west artery, is the "zero" for Miami's street numbers. Streets run east-west; avenues run north-south with **Miami Avenue** as the "zero." In the four quadrants thus created, streets and avenues are labelled NE, SE, SW, and NW. (See map of Miami and Miami Beach on the cover flaps).

The **Metro-Dade Cultural Center** (101 West Flagler Street), an arcaded building around a central plaza, was designed in post-modernist style by Philip Johnson. Under one roof are the **Center for the Fine Arts** (an art gallery and sculpture court with space for temporary exhibitions), an auditorium, Miami's central public library, and the **Historical Museum of Southern Florida**. The latter features dozens of hands-on displays. You can, for example, set the sails and haul the rigging on an old sailing boat — symbol of Florida's pioneer era.

Biscayne Boulevard, close to the waterfront, doubles as part of the circuit for Miami's Grand Prix and the route of the annual Orange Bowl Parade on New Year's Eve. The **Omni** centre, a huge shopping, entertainment, and hotel

Modern skyline of downtown Miami.

complex, occupies a stretch of boulevard frontage near the Venetian Causeway to Miami Beach.

Flagler Street meets Biscayne Boulevard and the Bay at Bayfront Park. The big draw here is **Bayside**, a waterfront complex of shops and eating places with its own pier, yacht berths, promenade, and free entertainment. North and across a drawbridge is the **Port of Miami**, home base for sleek cruise ships which sail the Caribbean.

Leaping killer whales entertain the crowd at Miami's Seaquarium.

South of Bayfront Park, Du Pont Plaza is home to the 5,000-seat **Miami Convention Center** and a number of hotels. Across the Miami River to the south, **Brickell Avenue**, the "Wall Street" of the South, is lined with high-rise office buildings and apartment complexes.

While **Little Havana** begins in downtown Miami, the centre of the district is a 30-block section stretching west along SW 8th Street called *Calle Ocho*. Restaurants here specialize in Cuban and other Latin American cuisine; street-side snack bars serve strong and aromatic *café cubano*. Lots of small businesses flourish in the area, too. It's estimated that over 600,000 Cubans now live in Miami, making them the largest ethnic group.

Key Biscayne

One of the earliest marine parks, the **Seaquarium** is reached by the Rickenbacker Causeway, "the steepest hill in Miami," which arcs over the bay towards the island of Key Biscayne. Compared with Sea World in Orlando, this one is showing its age, but has the merit that you are very close to the action.

Shows are timed so that spectators can move from one performance to the next to see shark-feeding, juggling sea lions, leaping killer whales, and basketball-playing dolphins, the "Miami Heatwave," (not to be confused with the local human team, the Miami Heat). These friendly performers live for a long time, but the dolphin named "Flipper" who stars here is a successor, not the original who had a TV show years ago.

The Seaquarium is one of the few places where you can see the rare manatee, or sea-cow, though you might be lucky and spot one in the wild. These seal-like mammals used to live in great numbers in Florida's waterways before the ad-

vent of the propeller-driven speed boats that killed many of them.

The northern part of Key Biscayne is given over to **Crandon Park**, a vast public beach with picnic facilities. Don't pick the sea oats that line the beach; they prevent erosion of the sand.

The southern end of the island is the **Bill Baggs State Recreation Area**, site of the 1825 Cape Florida lighthouse. Devastated by Hurricane Andrew in 1992,

The trendy village of Coconut Grove on the shores of Biscayne Bay.

most of the park has now reopened. The keeper's cottage was totally destroyed, but the lighthouse is still there and can be visited.

The "Gables" and the "Grove"

Southwest of the city centre, the wealthy community of **Coral Gables** is graced with fountains, tropical gardens, and Spanish architecture. The **Lowe Art Museum** on the University of Miami campus (1301 Stanford Drive) has collections of primitive and Native American art, 17th-century Spanish paintings, and 20th-century art, especially sculpture.

Coconut Grove is a lively village-cum-suburb on the shores of the bay, with cosy little shops, bikeways, open-air cafés, clubs, and live theatre. It dates back to the years before Miami existed — a few early buildings still survive, notably **The Barnacle**, built from timber salvaged from shipwrecks.

Down by the sheltered yacht harbour, the little Art Deco building which now serves as **Miami City Hall** started life as the terminal for Pan American's flying boats, which took off from the bay for Cuba and points south in the 1930s. In the late afternoon, stroll through the centre of the Grove, watching out for kamikaze rollerbladers slicing through the traffic — but don't stray too far to the west, a notoriously dangerous area.

At the Miami end of Coconut Grove, the Italianate palace of **Vizcaya** (3251 S. Miami Avenue) was built for the tractor magnate James Deering. An odd but imposing mixture of styles, it is decorated with tapestries, massive furniture, and Classical sculpture. Outside, elegant terraces sweep down to the bay, but the grounds also include dense jungle, left uncut at Deering's insistence. Follow the detailed Vizcaya guidebook when you tour the house.

Across South Miami Avenue, opposite Vizcaya, the **Museum of Science** features dozens of hands-on exhibits, while the adjacent **Space Transit Planetarium** screens a series of multi-media laser shows on various aspects of astronomy. The adjoining wildlife centre provides a secure home for injured birds of prey.

South of the City

South on Old Cutler Road, the lush **Fairchild Tropical Garden** comprises over 32 hectares (80 acres) of tropical plants, trees, shrubs, and flowers. Tram tours can take you round or you can stroll through the grounds on foot.

Exotic wildlife at the Metrozoo.

Near the park, just off 57th Avenue, the **Parrot Jungle's** macaws, flamingos, and other exotic birds are seemingly unrestricted. Parrots will eat out of your hand — you can feed them with approved seed dispensed by vending machines. Trained birds ride bicycles, roller-skate, and count, while the "Senior Psittacines," retired parrots of 50 years old and more, doze contentedly on their perches.

The cageless **Metrozoo**, south at 12400 SW 152nd Street, is one of the largest and most modern zoos in the United

States, home to white Bengal tigers, gorillas, giraffes, and elephants. The park can be toured on the monorail, which is back in operation after being badly damaged in the 1992 hurricane. The spectacular walk-through aviary, virtually destroyed in 1992, is in the process of being rebuilt. For information on the state of repairs call (305) 251-0400.

Right opposite the Metrozoo's main entrance, the **Gold Coast Railroad Museum** has collected a wide range of historic rolling stock. The prime exhibit is Presidential

Rail Car U.S. number 1, *Ferdinand Magellan*, converted for Franklin Roosevelt but put to use primarily by Harry Truman on a 28,000-

Brightly colored exotic birds entertain at the Parrot Jungle.

mile campaign tour in 1948; it is now a National Historic Landmark.

About an hour south of Miami, **Monkey Jungle** (at SW 216th Street) keeps human visitors caged while 500 other primates are free to swing, climb, and dive in the cultivated tropical jungle.

Biscayne National Park offers snorkelling, diving, and swimming over the coral reefs around Elliott Key and 23 attendant islets. From Convoy Point near Homestead, park boats take visitors over the coral reef.

THE GOLD COAST

At least five different roads lead north from Miami along this celebrated 70-mile (112-km) stretch of Atlantic coastline. The older highway U.S. 1 lies just inland from the coast; then comes I-95, the multi-lane Interstate, best if you want to travel fast; the Florida Turnpike toll road and U.S. 441 run farther inland than the others. Nearest to the sea is route A1A. For much of the way A1A links the barrier islands — there are some fabulous views along the way, but the many traffic lights can make it slow going.

This coastline includes half a dozen of Florida's most famous winter resorts, all with wide boulevards, white-painted banks, motels, hotels, condominiums, and restaurants. At first glance it's difficult to distinguish one place from another, but they all have enough individuality to inspire loyalty in their many regular visitors.

The first rather quiet resorts north of Miami are **Hallandale** and **Hollywood**, the latter more rural at its northern end. They're both favoured by older people, especially Canadians. **Dania**, north-west of Hollywood, is known locally as the antiques capital of Florida; all along U.S. 1 dealers have set up shops in the sunshine. Dania also has its own Jai Alai fronton.

Fort Lauderdale straddles more than 320 km (200 miles) of inland waterways lined with over 30,000 private boats and yachts. Most hotels and many motels face the beach, separated from it by the coast road. For an evening visit you can park in sight of the waves and make forays to restaurants across the highway.

The best way to get acquainted with the town is to take a ride on one of the rubber-wheeled sightseeing "trams." Guides give commentaries as the tour passes sumptuous waterfront homes, the car museum, orange groves, and the Seminole Village, where you can see alligator wrestling or play bingo for high stakes. (The self-administering Seminole nation can bypass state laws on gambling.)

For a complete change of scene, visit the **Museum of Art** (1 E. Las Olas Boulevard), with its strong, emphatically modern art and various ethnographic collections.

GOLD COAST

Ocean World on SE 17th Street entertains visitors with its dolphin and sea lion shows, tanks of sharks, turtles, reef fish, and alligators, as well as a number of caged monkeys and macaws.

Across the street from Ocean World, the misleadingly named Port Everglades is a major terminal for cruise ships and freighters. All sorts of **excursion cruises** start from Fort Lauderdale, some going as far as the Bahamas. Mississippi-style paddle-boats take regular daytime trips to the mangrove swamps and dinner cruises along the Intra-Coastal Waterway.

North from Fort Lauderdale, **Pompano Beach** is lined with towering condominiums, and is well known for the trotting races held at Pompano Park. Expensive parking keeps the beach quieter at **Boca Raton**, where as many people fish from the shore as take to the water. Boca claims to be the "Winter Polo Capital of the World." The sport is played on Sundays between January and April.

North past the apartments and golf clubs of Delray Beach brings you to **Lake Worth**. Casino Park Beach, a stretch of sloping sand next to Kreusler Memorial Park, sometimes has good waves for surfing. The **Museum of Art** (601 Lake Avenue) houses exhibitions in a converted Art Deco cinema.

PALM BEACH TO ST. AUGUSTINE

Palm Beach

Beautiful Italianate homes are half hidden behind walls and sculptured hedges here, in one of America's wealthiest communities. Some of the houses crowded along the 8-km (5-mile) strip of land are used only for a few weeks each winter, while the rest of the year they lie empty. Others may be rented to visitors. Drive along A1A to admire the landscape gardening and see how the rich arrange things when they get the chance. From Christmas to the end of February it's hard to park, or even to stop; at other times Palm Beach can be very quiet. The beach itself is narrow, since storms have eroded much of it.

For another glimpse of the good life, stroll along glamorous **Worth Avenue** amid Mediterranean-style buildings from the 1920s with palm-filled courtyards and elegant shops and restaurants. It all makes Beverly Hills' Rodeo Drive look comparatively

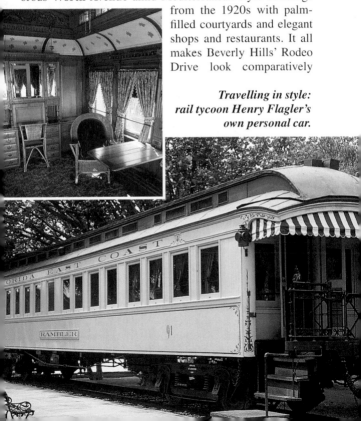

Travelling in style: rail tycoon Henry Flagler's own personal car.

down-market. Plays straight from Broadway come to spend the winter at the Royal Poinciana Playhouse.

The **Henry Morrison Flagler Museum** on Coconut Row, formerly the rail tycoon's extravagant 1901 mansion known as "Whitehall," retains some original furniture and photographs. Flagler's own railway carriage is parked in the garden, complete with copper-lined shower and cast-iron stove.

Across the causeway, **West Palm Beach** has the motels, businesses, light industry, and international airport which its well-groomed neighbour wasn't prepared to accommodate. The **Norton Gallery of Art** on U.S. 1 (1451 S. Olive Avenue) has a splendid collection of French Impressionists and Post-impressionists, including Gauguin's *The Agony in the Garden* as well as some fine Chinese jade.

From West Palm Beach, the causeway at Blue Heron Boulevard leads across to Palm Beach Shores, a new development of hotels and motels with a variety of leisure facilities. Inland at **Lion Country Safari** you can drive through herds of elephants and zebras, past lions and ostriches. If you come in a convertible, you'll have to swap it for one of the park's cars. The area labelled the Gold Coast ends at West Palm Beach. Under different names (Treasure Coast, Space Coast, and First Coast), the Florida beaches continue for another 480 km (300 miles) north to the state border.

Treasure Coast acquired its name from the Spanish ships which were wrecked along it, spilling their cargoes of gold and silver. (But truth to tell, any part of Florida's Atlantic seaboard could make the same claim.) Once a mangrove swamp with offshore sandbars, much of it is a long string of islands separated from the mainland by a saltwater strip called Indian River or Indian Creek. The leisurely route A1A connects the islands and resorts, frequently crossing bridges where Indian River is linked to the ocean by inlets.

The **Jonathan Dickenson State Park**, 20 km (13 miles) south of Stuart, provides vacation cabins, hookups for campers, and facilities for fishing, swimming, boating, canoeing, and hiking. **Jupiter Beach** to the south and Jupiter Island to the north are largely unbuilt-up, and there's plenty of free parking. Between Fort Pierce and Melbourne, sand dunes, shell shops, motels, and the occasional steakhouse are the main features of the landscape.

Space Coast

A nature reserve with alligators, eagles, and armadillos shares **Merritt Island** with scented orange groves and with NASA (the National Aeronautics and Space Administration). Here, at Cape Canaveral, the United States began to send rockets into space in the 1950s.

Nearby, the **John F. Kennedy Space Center** has been the launch site for American manned exploration of space, in-

Watch the spectacular blast off of space shuttles at the J. F. K. Space Center.

cluding the first mission to land a man on the moon in 1969. Now it's the base of the space shuttles. To find out when the next take-off is scheduled, check the daily papers. Whether there's a launch or not, it's well worth visiting the Spaceport, just off NASA Causeway linking A1A and U.S. 1. Expect to spend at least half a day.

The "Rocket Garden" includes the kind of launchers that put the first Americans into space, it's remarkable how small they look now. The **Astronauts' Memorial** honours those killed in the space programme. An appropriate blend of technology and sculpture, it turns with the sun and reflects light behind their names. Multimedia shows and exhibits explain the amazing technology of space travel, and a small lump of real moon rock is on show.

On the **Red Bus Tour** (schedule may vary for operational reasons), you'll be shown the highlights of the moon-landing programme. This includes the gigantic 158-meter (520-ft) VAB (Vehicle Assembly Building), a huge Saturn moon rocket, the moon launch pad, and mission control. The Blue

---

Last Fling for Old Hardware

When President Kennedy declared in 1961 that the U.S. would put a man on the moon (and bring him back) before the decade was out, no one knew how it could be achieved. Everything had to be designed and built from scratch. What is so striking now, apart from the colossal size of the multi-stage Saturn launcher and the sheer daring of those who rode on its nose, is the old-fashioned "nuts and bolts" appearance of it all. It looks like World War II equipment and with reason. The engineers were taking enough chances as it was, so they built what they knew. Despite today's vaunted technology, one has to wonder if the will, the courage, and the money could be summoned up to do the job now or ever again.

Bus Tour is more for rocket buffs — it deals with the unmanned programme. The **IMAX films** shown on five-storey high screens are thrilling: *The Dream is Alive*, also shown at the Air & Space Museum in Washington, D.C., is the story of the space shuttle; *L5: First City in Space* is a dazzling vision of the future. Allow at least half a day for a visit.

East of the spaceport, Port Canaveral is the newest of Florida's cruise terminals. If your holiday combines Orlando with a cruise, your ship will probably leave from here.

Cocoa Beach, on the narrow island strip to the south, was tiny when the first astronauts came here to relax from their training. Now it's a growing resort, a favourite among surfers and teenagers who jam its sands near the old wooden pier. The dunes are a great vantage point for watching space launches.

Some 80 km (50 miles) north of Cape Canaveral near New Smyrna Beach is the inlet where Ponce de León, credited as the discoverer of Florida, stepped ashore in 1513.

Then comes the "World's Most Famous Beach," as **Daytona Beach** proudly proclaims itself. Its 37 km (23 miles) of hard-packed sand doubles as a roadway for a $3 toll, although every so often a stalled car gets caught by the tide. The 16 km/h (10 mph) speed limit hardly recalls the roaring twenties and thirties when Sir Henry Segrave and Sir Malcolm Campbell set world land speed records here, culminating in Campbell's 444 km/h (276 mph) in 1935.

The flat sands, lifeguard towers, and shallow water make the beach safe for children. And, like every Florida beach, it's most perfect at dawn, when early joggers scarcely bother the myriad sea birds and waders.

On 4 July each year, the annual 400-mile (645-km) Daytona 500 stock-car race is held at the **Daytona International Speedway**. The event is usually scheduled for late February. An entire car and motorcycle culture has grown up around the track, with parades, flea markets, and special events. Hot rodders and bikers in black leather cruise the streets and burn rubber at the traffic lights.

Inland Excursion

A trip to Lake George and Ocala National Forest is worth the drive westwards from Ormond Beach. Off Highway 40 at Juniper Springs, warm clear water surges out of the ground to form a natural swimming pool. There are other spa-resorts, notably Alexander Springs to the south of the forest and **Silver Springs** on its western edge. Here you can view a menagerie of animals from a safari boat, or spot fish and underwater plants through the floor of a glass-bottomed boat. Elsewhere on the grounds are a reptile institute, waterslides, and a collection of antique cars.

Route 19 through the **Ocala National Forest**, itself a sizable wilderness of lakes, hills, and springs, offers first-class camping, hiking, and fishing. To the west is the town of Ocala, and, 56 km (35 miles) to the northwest, the university city of Gainsville.

First Coast is the label given to the northern end of Florida's Atlantic seaboard, site of the earliest European settlements in the region. Dolphins and whales leaping and cavorting in the water can be seen at **Marineland**, where the idea of sea-life parks began. Dating from the

Dolphins perform spectacular acrobatics at Marineland.

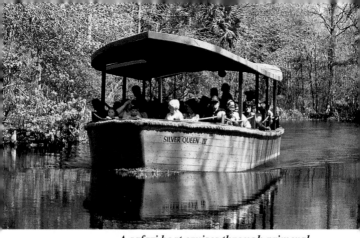

A safari boat cruises through primeval jungle in Silver Springs.

1930s, it grew into a resort, but the buildings are now showing their age and newer parks have left it behind.

St. Augustine

You'll come to shrug off superlatives in Florida, but this really *is* the oldest city in the United States (founded in 1565, long before the *Mayflower*). Its Spanish architecture, churches, and distinctly colonial atmosphere make it unlike anywhere else in Florida.

Most striking of the buildings is the **Castillo de San Marcos**, a star-shaped Spanish fortress started in 1672 as a response to repeated raids by pirates and the English (in some cases there was no clear distinction betwen the two categories). Completed in 1695, its fortified walls, up to 3.7 metres (12 feet) thick in places, are built of *coquina*, a stone formed of naturally bonded seashells and so effective at absorbing bombardment that the fortress never fell to assault. Exhibits and recreations of the historical events connected with the fort are presented daily. (See page 121.)

A sightseeing road-train will take you on a tour of the historic old city, and then you can return to landmarks such as the well-restored **Oldest House** or the **Oldest Store Museum**. This turn-of-the-century emporium is stocked with 100,000 authentic items from that period, many of them accidentally discovered in a warehouse attic. You can see old buttoned shoes and lace corsets, toys, groceries, medicines, bonnets, bicycles, hats, and guns.

Henry Flagler built the imposing Ponce de León Hotel for the new wave of tourists when his railroad reached St. Augustine in 1888. Now, it houses Flagler College. If you can, take a look inside the rotunda, the former hotel lobby. Outside again, notice the early use of poured concrete, strangely allied with

The 19th-century Ponce de León Hotel in St. Augustine, built by railway baron Henry Flagler.

such decorative architecture. Across the street, another Flagler hotel is now the **Lightner Museum**, a collection of Victoriana, Tiffany glass, and 19th-century musical instruments. A third former hotel on the square makes an impressive City Hall. On summer evenings at the amphitheatre, the city's founding is re-enacted in an outdoor pageant, "Cross and Sword."

ORLANDO AND CENTRAL FLORIDA

Now the largest city in central Florida, **Orlando** entered the tourism business in a big way when Walt Disney World moved in down the road. The huge number of hotel rooms in the area now means that Orlando can accommodate the biggest conventions and sports events and Central Florida offers the world's greatest collection of purpose-built attractions.

Many visitors to the area stay at or near Disney World or on International Drive and never venture into downtown Orlando, which is a pity. It's hard to tell what has been restored and what is brand-new at **Church Street Station**, a complex of fun shopping, food, and entertainment. It's all open during the day, but after about 5:30 P.M. you have to pay to get in. There may be a dozen shows to choose from — ranging from jazz bands to cancan girls to elegant Country and Western opera across the street at the Cheyenne Saloon. (The gambling here is only "pretend.") Street entertainers, pubs, and restaurants add to the downtown diversions.

International Drive, 19 km (12 miles) away and as far again from Disney World, has grown from nothing in just a few years. Entirely a creation of the tourist boom, it's a glitzy strip of hotels, fast-food outlets, bars, and all-you-can-eat buffets.

In the years before Disney, **Kissimmee** was a sleepy town where the local cattle ranchers might drop in once a week. Now, it's hard to find the old centre, amid miles and miles of motels, T-shirt "factory outlets," and "British" pubs. If you persist, you'll find it along Main Street and Broadway, where nothing much has changed. The town still holds a cattle market, and a rodeo twice a year.

The **Flying Tigers Warbirds Air Museum** at the local airport has a collection of rare old planes in various stages of restoration. You can take a flight in an open biplane or in the airship you'll see cruising overhead when you're in the theme parks.

☞ Walt Disney World

Tens of millions of people come every year to Walt Disney World, the most popular tourist attraction on earth, lying 32 km (20 miles) southwest of Orlando off Interstate 4 and U.S. 192. It's not just one theme park, but three, and an immense holiday resort with dozens of hotels, a camp-ground, five golf courses, aquaparks, tennis courts, vaca-tion villas, and shops. Statistics show that 80 percent of all the visitors are adults, although for the purposes of Disney ticket sales, adulthood be-gins at the age of 10. Dis-ney World has even become America's favourite honey-moon destination. In all, the site covers some 11,000 hectares (28,000 acres), roughly twice the area of Manhattan Island.

Flavour of the Wild West at the Cheyenne Saloon in Orlando.

Visitors to Disney World generally divide their time among the **Magic Kingdom**, the **Disney-MGM Studios,** and the nearby **EPCOT Cen-ter**. Yet another attraction,

Disney's Animal Kingdom, opens in 1998. A day for each is hardly enough, and if you stay longer, there are still more major attractions within the Disney area, including Blizzard Beach, Typhoon Lagoon, and River Country (water adventure parks) and Pleasure Island (bars, night-clubs, and live entertainment). To encourage you, there are money-saving 4-day and 5-day passes as well as one-day, one-park tickets. (See page 119 for approximate prices. They may seem expensive, but, once inside, all rides and attractions are free.) Several tour companies operate excursions — travel agents can give you details of what's available.

Fairy-tales come alive at the Magic Castle.

The Magic Kingdom

From the Ticket and Transportation Center, take the sleek monorail or a ferryboat across the lake. (Buses for Disney hotel guests go straight to the entrance.) The Magic Kingdom is divided into seven different "lands." Stroll from one to the next, but not too slowly — there's a lot to see and do.

Main Street USA. Just beyond the entrance, you pass beneath Main Street Railroad Station into Town Square. **City Hall**, to your left, is the place for information about any aspect of Disney World. The square is always filled with life, and sometimes a crowd clusters round one of the Disney characters (they'll sign autographs but they don't speak).

Ahead of you, buildings in early 20th-century style line Main Street. Soon you'll see an antique double-decker bus or horse-drawn tram. You'll want to stop at the shops, but try to be at the other end by 9:00 A.M. when the other lands open.

At the end of the street and across a bridge, a circular **Plaza** is backed by **Cinderella Castle**, the pinnacled symbol of the Magic Kingdom. Radial routes lead from here to all the "lands." Our description proceeds clockwise, but don't follow any formula too strictly. Pick out things that appeal to you.

Adventureland. First you'll spot the giant banyan tree which supports the **Swiss Family Treehouse.** For all its woody appearance, it's actually made of concrete and vinyl. Just be-

---

Tips for Touring Disney World

1. Pick your parks. If it's your first visit and you have three days or more, leave the Magic Kingdom for the second or third. If you have only one, choose the Magic Kingdom, which is the essence of Disney's fantasy.

2. **Arrive early** to get your money's worth and beat the crowd to the most popular rides. The official opening time is 9 a.m., but Main Street USA is open at 8 a.m. and EPCOT and Disney-MGM Studios open their gates at about 8:30 a.m.

3. Make a note of where you leave your car in the huge parks.

4. Pick up a **free guidebook and map**, and an entertainment schedule, and plan a route.

5. Rides last 5 to 15 minutes or so. Access is cleverly controlled, and huge numbers of people can be accommodated, 3,000 an hour or more on some rides. The wait time is predicted on signs or by the hosts. You may avoid some lines by starting with rides more distant from the entrance and working back.

yond, you can board boats for the **Jungle Cruise** or join **Pirates of the Caribbean** for a voyage to their treasure trove.

Frontierland celebrates America's Old West, both real and legendary. Take aim at the old-time Shootin' Gallery, go for a roller-coaster ride through Gold Rush days on the **Big Thunder Mountain Railroad**, board an elegant triple-decker or raft across to Tom Sawyer Island. The **Diamond Horseshoe Jamboree** is a live show in Wild West style. (Book seats at the Disneyana Collectibles store in Town Square.) Newest and most popular of the rides here is **Splash Mountain**. Your boat will seem to hang interminably in space before dropping five storeys into a pool.

Liberty Square. A few steps away, the architecture changes from Old West to New England. The **Hall of Presidents** is a major attraction, with America's leaders brought to life through *Audio-Animatronics*. Even though you know the performers are mechanical replicas, the moment will come when you'll feel you're listening to Washington and Lincoln. The **Haunted Mansion** nearby is more funny than frightening, even when one of its 999 ghosts comes to sit next to you.

Fantasyland. The Magic Kingdom is fantasy throughout, but here it's in the purest form. The **Mad Tea Party** is a good place to begin, with a dizzying whirl in a gigantic teacup. **It's a Small World** sets everyone smiling as they cruise past singing, dancing dolls. Small children adore **Dumbo the Flying Elephant** and **Cinderella's Golden Carrousel**, a classic merry-go-round.

From Fantasyland, you can take the **Skyway** cable car to Tomorrowland or walk through Cinderella Castle past fine mosaics of scenes from the Disney film *Cinderella*.

Mickey's Toontown Fair. Newest of the lands, this one is tucked away, so you could easily miss it. Mickey's House is set up like a museum of memorabilia, but it is at **Toontown**

*Experience new-age- technology and
cultural diversity at the Epcot Center.*

County Fair where you'll meet the Mouse himself, ready to sign autographs and pose for pictures.

Tomorrowland is dominated by a white cone of steel, the famous **Space Mountain**. Inside, a thrilling roller-coaster ride races through inky blackness. Be sure to heed the warning signs, and don't attempt the ride if you've got a weak neck, back, heart, or stomach. A less nerve-frazzling option is the **WEDWay PeopleMover**, where little cars float on an electromagnetic cushion. Two popular new attractions are **The Timekeeper**, a brilliant simulation of time travel narrated by actor Robin Williams, and **Alien Encounter**, featuring a bevvy of extraterrestrials.

Dreamflight traces aviation's history, and in **Grand Prix Cars Raceway** you can control the speed, but guiderails stop the race from turning into chaos.

Before leaving the Magic Kingdom, take a trip round its borders on the **Walt Disney World Railroad**. The four narrow-gauge steam locomotives which haul the open passenger cars are the real thing. Built in Philadelphia between 1916 and 1928, they were discovered, still hard at work, in Mexico's Yucatan Peninsula in the 1960s.

EPCOT Center

Twenty years in the planning and opened in 1982, Walt Disney World's "Experimental Prototype Community of Tomorrow" is a park full of attractions to enlighten and entertain with all manner of special effects and computerized gadgetry.

The park has two distinct theme areas, together forming a figure 8. In the first, **Future World**, the pavilions are sponsored by some of America's biggest corporations such as General Motors, Exxon, and Kodak. The second, **World Showcase**, celebrates the cultures and products of eleven different nations. EPCOT is reached by car and shuttle bus and from the Magic Kingdom by monorail. The hottest new attraction at EPCOT, the **Test Track**, is also its most thrilling ride. In this simulation of an automotive proving ground, six people ride a test car through a high-speed hill climb and over banked curves.

Future World

The great white sphere near the main entrance is **Spaceship Earth**, the symbol of EPCOT. Inside it, a spectacular ride spirals up through scenes depicting the development of communications. Near its base, **Earth Station** is an information centre.

Straight ahead lie the twin buildings of **Innovations, East and West**, where you can sample such high-tech gadgetry as a wrist telephone, virtual reality, and state-of-the-art video games. Grouped around Communicore are the main attractions of Future World. We take a clockwise route, but you'll need to be flexible depending on the length of the queues.

The **Universe of Energy** show is presented in a travelling theatre; the seats actually move, powered in part by solar cells on the roof of the building. A spectacular film about energy sources is followed by a trip through scenes dramatizing the formation of fossil fuels, complete with Audio-Animatronic dinosaurs and primeval mist.

The **Wonders of Life** include the hilarious *Cranium Command*, putting you inside the head of a boy as he faces the crises of a school day. *The Making of Me*, a funny but serious film, illustrates human reproduction and birth. There's always a rush to *Body Wars*, a thrilling flight-simulator ride where you're "shrunk" and sent rushing through arteries, veins, heart, and lungs.

Center Court is where you can analyze your golf swing or count your calorie expenditure after a brief workout. **Des-**

tinations includes a farm where robots harvest crops and colonies under the sea and in space.

The **GM World of Motion**, in a suitably wheel-shaped building, takes you on a ride through the history of transport from cave-dwellers, past old coaches and cars, to the city of tomorrow.

Journey into Imagination goes on a whimsical journey through the creative process in the company of a couple of characters called Dreamfinder and Figment. In the same pavilion is *Honey, I Shrunk the Kids*, a wild 3-D adventure that convincingly simulates the microscopic experience.

The Land focuses on food and other useful crops. In *Listen to the Land* you cruise by boat past experimental fish farms and through greenhouses where plants grow in sand or suspended in air. If you are especially interested, sign up for a 45-minute walking tour.

The Living Seas exhibit features an underwater ride to the biggest artificial coral reef in the world, stocked with a variety of marine life from dolphins to barracuda. In the Coral Reef restaurant, you can dine alongside these underwater wonders.

World Showcase

Ranged round the perimeter of a lagoon stand replicas of some of the world's great monuments. A scale model of the Eiffel Tower rises above the Florida landscape; a diminutive version of Venice's Campanile stands near a Mayan pyramid from Mexico, and so on. Eleven nations are represented, all with restaurants featuring the national cuisine.

Mexico's pyramid houses priceless pre-Columbian treasures and a riverboat trip through Mexican history.

Norway offers a boat trip on the stormy *Maelstrom*. The Akershus restaurant puts on a typical Norwegian buffet.

China's circular Temple of Heaven is just right for the film *Wonders of China*.

Germany concentrates on traditional food and beer, and shops selling fine glass, silver, porcelain, chocolates, and wine.

Italy also emphasizes eating and drinking, in a branch of L'Originale Alfredo di Roma. Street performers entertain the crowds in "St. Mark's Square."

The United States takes centre stage. *The American Adventure* takes a half-hour journey through American history in film and special effects, including some of the most life-like Audio-Animatronics figures yet made by Disney.

Japan shows a formal face, with tranquil gardens and temples. Four eating places serve Japanese dishes, and there's a branch of a famous Tokyo department store.

Morocco's authentic buildings are a World Showcase highlight. They house a colourful bazaar and the Restaurant Marrakesh, where a belly dancer diverts the diners.

France concentrates on gastronomy in three French restaurants each with an all-French staff. Don't miss the big-screen film *Impressions de France*.

The United Kingdom cultivates an "olde worlde" image with Tudor buildings and the Rose and Crown Pub and Dining Room.

Canada shows a Circle-Vision 360 film, Inuit (Eskimo) and Indian crafts are featured in the shops.

Disney-MGM Studios

Celebrating the American love affair with the movies, the newest of the Disney World theme parks opened, a mile southwest of EPCOT in 1989. They really do make films and TV programmes here, but above all it's fun. The streets are full of all kinds of happenings and surprises, so here we mention only some of the highlights.

Inside the entrance, leave the shops until later and walk down **Hollywood Boulevard** towards the big open space of Sunset Plaza. On the right you'll see a giant **clapperboard** chalked with all the latest information on shows and waiting times. Nearby, the open-air **Theater of the Stars** stages a live musical based on Disney's hit *Beauty and the Beast*.

Many who arrive as the gates open run to a ride or show that will have long lines later. **The Twilight Zone Tower of Terror** is the place for those who enjoy 13-storey drops through pitch darkness. **Star Tours**, a simulator thrill created by George Lucas in the tradition of *Star Wars*, takes place on an imaginary but all-too-convincing trip to Endor, where you're thrown around while a synchronized 70-mm film shows the frightening view from the out-of-control space-craft. Those in the know then head straight for the **Indiana Jones Stunt Spectacular**. The name says it all.

In **The Great Movie Ride**, your seats carry you through animated scenes from *Casablanca*, *The Wizard of Oz*, *Alien,* and a dozen more landmark films. Disney-MGM is now the official home of **The Muppets**, the late Jim Henson's inspired creations, and you can see them "on set" in the street or in a remarkable 3-D film. **Voyage of the Little Mermaid** is a multi-media show based on the Disney film — be prepared to get splashed!

Check the daily attractions at Disney-MGM Studios.

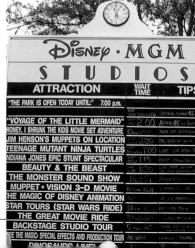

Confronting the jaws of death at Universal Studios.

The **Backstage Tours** shouldn't be missed. **Studio Tour** takes you on a shuttle ride past costuming, scene-building, and props departments. Next, **Catastrophe Canyon** is where "by mistake" you get mixed up in a disaster movie complete with earthquake, explosions, fires, and a flash flood. When you've recovered, you can walk through the **Special Effects and Production Tour**. Before 5:00 P.M. or so, when the artists pack up work for the day, go to **The Magic of Disney Animation** for a walking tour which will give you an insight into the intricate process by which animated films are made.

Pleasure Island

Conscious that they were losing guests in the evenings to the attractions of downtown Orlando and elsewhere, the Disney organization decided to create some nightlife of its own. This is the result, a complex of bars and dance halls, a Comedy Warehouse, clubs, and live bands on an open-air stage. The setting is the abandoned, ramshackle old warehouses of some run-down port all specially built in 1989. There's an entrance fee in the evening, but it's free during the day.

More Attractions at Walt Disney World

Typhoon Lagoon is a giant aquapark with beaches, water-slides, and streams where you can drift along sitting in a rubber ring. Its claim to fame, though, is a huge lagoon where the world's biggest wave-making machine generates rollers up to 1.8 metres (six feet) high for body-surfing.

The older **River Country** has more waterslides, a lakeside beach, white-water rapids, and ropes and bridges for swinging and dropping into the "old swimming hole."

Across the water from here, **Discovery Island** is a nature sanctuary with boardwalks meandering past the exotic plant and bird life. They've had some successes here with the breeding of endangered species.

Blizzard Beach the newest of Disney's three waterparks, is based on an abandoned ski resort and features the tallest free-fall water slide in the world.

For more information about Disney events, accommodation, prices, and packages, contact Walt Disney World, Box 10,000, Lake Buena Vista, FL 32830. Tel. (407) 824-4321.

Other Theme Parks in Central Florida

Universal Studios

Over 160 hectares (400 acres) of realistic sets — San Francisco waterfront, New York streets, Hollywood — and real production equipment make this the biggest facility of its kind east of California. Arrive early if you can, collect a map at the gate, and plan a route.

When it opened in 1990, comparisons were inevitably made with Disney-MGM Studios. Universal tends to be less whimsical, perhaps appealing more to teenagers and film buffs than to small children, though even they can't get enough of Yogi Bear and Fred Flintstone in **The Funtastic World of Hanna-Barbera**. Because the area is a lot bigger here than at Disney, the streets may be less crowded, and at times it can seem there is less going on. But Universal Studios can claim four of the most thrilling rides anywhere. The newest is **Terminator 2 3-D**, where you'll find yourself alongside Arnold Schwarzenegger, dodging laser fire in a cyber battle. In **Kongfrontation**, the mighty King Kong, five storeys high, has escaped and is rampaging through New York. You are riding a cable car above a city street when Kong attacks…

Earthquake puts you in a San Francisco subway train, standing peacefully at a station when all hell breaks loose — the effects have actually been measured at 8.3 on the Richter scale. The roof collapses, a truck rolls straight at

Flamingos are one of Florida's native species.

you, water floods in. It's a relief when the director finally shouts "Cut!"

Virtual reality takes a great leap forward in **Back to the Future**, a ride vaguely based on the films of that name. You chase through space while an advanced flight simulator convinces you that you're diving out of control, backed by the evidence of amazing images on the huge wrap-around screen.

A Wild West stunt show, adventures based on *ET* and *Ghostbusters*, Alfred Hitchcock's secrets, lessons on gruesome make-up, and a backlot "tram tour" provide more than enough to fill a day.

Sea World

Close to International Drive, is the leader in Florida's marine parks. They'll give you a map and an up-to-date schedule of events, specially printed out, as you enter, so you can plan your visit. Check the times of the shows: highlights include performing dolphins and sea lions; Shamu, the friendly killer whale, propelling a trainer out of the water like a Polaris missile; polar bears cavorting in an icy Arctic playground; and waterskiing displays. Between times, visit the seals, or the penguins in their great glass-sided tank refrigerated to the sort of chill they prefer.

In one remarkable exhibit, "Terrors of the Deep," you walk through a tank full of sharks in a transparent tunnel. Sea World claims to have "more of everything," including Polynesian dancers, Chinese acrobats, and several restaurants. The ride to the top of the 120-metre (400-foot) Sky Tower costs a little extra, but is worth it for the view.

Wet "n" Wild

This collection of lakes and pools, off International Drive (it's closed in winter and bad weather), is equipped with

A boat ride is one way to soak in the glorious sights at Cypress Gardens.

water-slides, rapids, a wave machine, and other sports facilities where you can cool off on a scorching day.

Cypress Gardens

South of Orlando, near Winter Haven, this lakeside park began as a botanic garden in the 1930s. Now it's more famous for the spectacular daily shows on the lake by waterskiers performing acrobatics and forming human pyramids. On shore, Southern Crossroads is a replica of an old southern town (circa 1900) with shops and restaurants. You can ride an electric boat or stroll through the remarkable gardens, home to 8,000 species of plants. The 46-metre (153-foot-) high Kodak Island in the Sky raises and lowers its passengers every few minutes for a panoramic view of the surroundings.

Nearby **Lake Wales** offers a winter home for the North Dakota Black Hills Passion Play. From February to April each year, the huge cast performs the last seven days in the life of Christ in an amphitheatre two miles out of town. The **Bok Singing Tower** is an elegant belfry blending Gothic and Art Nouveau, set in quiet gardens on Central Florida's highest hill. Every day at 3:00 P.M. the resident musician plays a recital on the 57-bell carillon. If you miss it there's a short recorded excerpt every 30 minutes.

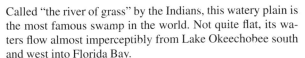

THE EVERGLADES

Called "the river of grass" by the Indians, this watery plain is the most famous swamp in the world. Not quite flat, its waters flow almost imperceptibly from Lake Okeechobee south and west into Florida Bay.

The 560,000-hectare (1,400,000-acre) **Everglades National Park** is a protected area of marshy land and broken coastline. Winter, the dry season, is the ideal time to visit. You'll see most bird life then, and there are fewer mosquitoes. Any time you visit, remember that this fragile ecosystem is being fiercely defended against encroaching development by environmentalists around the world. For

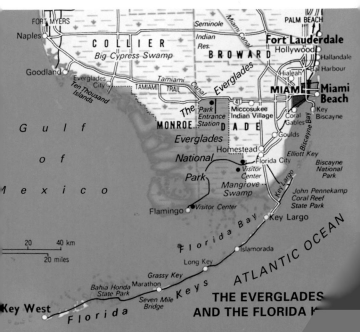

THE EVERGLADES
AND THE FLORIDA K

maps and literature, write to Everglades National Park, 40001 State Road 9336, Homestead, FL 33034-6733.

From Miami head south to Homestead, then take State Road 27 and watch for signs to the park. Soon you'll come to the park entrance station, where you can pick up an excellent free map. The park road winds for 61 km (38 miles) to the coast. Several marked turnoffs along the way take you to campsites and picnic grounds beside lakes or near "hammocks" — raised, usually wooded areas in the swamps.

The first turnoff leads to the **Royal Palm Visitor Center**, on the edge of a freshwater slough (pronounced "slew"). Look down into the clear wa-

Alligators abound in the Florida Everglades.

ters of the pond to see shoals of fish, including the Florida garfish, one of the principal foods of the alligator. There are brief slide-shows on the Everglades, and the resident rangers will suggest where you should go. The Anhinga Trail's board-walk circles over the sawgrass marsh. Look for alligators, egrets, herons, and the anhinga, or snake-bird, which swims under water with its snake-like neck protruding, and then sits in a bush raising its wings to dry. The Gumbo Limbo Trail is the other circular half-mile track. Look out for raccoons, opossums, tree-snails, and lizards.

Back on the road you'll pass several more trails and sight-seeing points, all marked on the park map, before you reach **Flamingo**, a fishing village on a shallow bay, with a colour-ful history of illicit liquor ("moonshine") production. Now life revolves around a ranger station, a lodge, a campground, restaurant, and grocery store. At Flamingo Marina you can buy bait and rent tackle, boats, and canoes.

Sightseeing boats take trips from Flamingo, and canoeists find their own way up to Everglades City through a chain of lakes and rivers called "The Wilderness Waterway." Look out for great white herons, snowy egrets, roseate spoonbills, ospreys, and southern bald eagles. Take plenty of insect re-pellent, especially in summer. Hunting and firearms are banned, but fishing is permitted.

Another entrance to the park lies off the Tamiami Trail (U.S. 41), which crosses the state from Miami to Naples. Signs all along the trail promote them, but Coopertown is the centre for **airboat rides**. Flat-bottomed boats powered by aeroplane propellers will take you sliding over swamp and shooting between clumps of sawgrass. (Airboats are banned in the National Park.)

At the **Miccosukee Indian Village** you can see crafts de-monstrations and some rather uninspiring alligator wrestl-

*Traditional Indian craftwork at the Miccosukee
Village in Everglades National Park.*

ing. The Miccosukee have lived in isolation here since the
time of the Seminole war, but fewer than 100 were left when
the U.S. government recognized the tribe in 1962. Now there
are over 500. Beyond the village, the Tamiami Trail passes
along the southern perimeter of the Big Cypress National
Preserve.

The western gateway to the National Park is **Everglades
City**, the site of another ranger station, where you can take
leisurely cruises among the "10,000 islands" spotting
wildlife. This is still one of the world's largest remaining
areas of mangrove forest, although seriously depleted. Pre-
serving what remains is not just conservation for the sake of
it: this environment is essential as the breeding ground of
commercially important species of fish.

THE FLORIDA KEYS

Curving westward from below Miami, a chain of islands
called the Keys, 190 km (120 miles) long, is stitched together

by 43 bridges and the world's longest ocean-going road. First built as the last stage of Flagler's East Coast Railroad, the **Overseas Highway** soars and leapfrogs out to the old naval town of Key West.

South from Homestead follow Highway 1, or take the quieter Card Sound Road, through 50 km (30 miles) of flat swampland where herons and storks have built their great untidy nests of sticks on the telephone poles. You'll soon be on **Key Largo**, largest of the islands. The southern end is a ribbon of the uglier sort of commercial development, but it's the base for trips to the **John Pennekamp State Park**, 43 km (27 miles) of coral reefs, tropical fish, sponges, and shipwrecks. Plenty of small shops rent diving equipment, cameras, and boats. To scuba dive you need to be qualified; there are schools here where you can sign up and pay tuition for lessons. Glass-bottomed boats make regular trips along the reef for those who prefer to keep dry while admiring the fish. (Take an anti-seasickness pill if it's rough weather and you are susceptible.)

Moored at Mile Marker 100 (locations on the Keys are expressed in distances from Key West), the little steamboat *African Queen* was built in England in 1912 and used on Lake Albert in East Africa. She appears in the 1951 film starring Humphrey Bogart and Katherine Hepburn. Strictly speaking, though, she has no business to be here — Bogart didn't even make *Key Largo* on Key Largo.

Farther down the Keys on the group of islands called **Islamorada**, you'll find plenty of opportunities for diving and snorkelling, as well as fishing for some of the estimated 600 species of fish. At one of the oldest marine shows in Florida, **Theater of the Sea**, cheerful young trainers lead visitors from one pool to another, pointing out dolphins, rays, sharks, and sea lions.

Building Bridges

At many places along the way you'll see where the old Flagler railway viaducts were converted into a roadway after a hurricane destroyed several sections in 1935. Some abandoned sections of bridge make superb fishing piers, if you can keep the pelican competition at bay. The **Long Key Viaduct**, 3 km (2 miles) long, is one of the most striking achievements of the railway builders, and Long Key itself has a state park and campground.

Marathon, chief town of the Middle Keys, is a sizeable resort and a diving and fishing centre. The museum is informative on the geology of the Keys and their early inhabitants. After Marathon, Flagler's engineers met their biggest challenge: 11 km (7 miles) of sea to be bridged on the way to the Lower Keys. The **Seven-Mile Bridge** still stands, a monument to the hundreds of workers who died between 1905 and

Don't Touch

A coral reef is alive and growing, the creation of billions of tiny polyps. Related to jellyfish and sea anemones, these little animals live in cup-shaped shells of limestone that they build for themselves. Coral's gorgeous colours come from algae living within the coral tissue. Each new generation builds on the skeletons of the last, but the outer living layer is thin and very fragile. A boat's anchor can leave a dead white scar. Even the touch of a diver's hand or foot can spread decay. In shallower water, corals resemble boulders and delicate fans. Farther out, where they have to stand up to a battering from waves, come the branching elkhorn varieties. Even from a glass-bottom boat you'll see hosts of fish enjoying the reef's protection. Their bright colours probably relate to the need to distinguish foes from possible mates in the crowd.

1912, the time it took to build the Overseas Railroad. Now it's defunct, replaced by a new road bridge with parapets frustratingly blocking the view. Stop at either end to see the bridges sweep over turquoise water into the misty distance.

Bahia Honda, a state recreation area and nature reserve, has a tropical sandy beach, something of a rarity in the Keys. You'll notice the strange double-decker bridge here: the road used to be on top.

At last Highway 1, which follows the entire East Coast for 3,200 km (2,000 miles), can go no farther; you've reached the remote town of Key West, which has become as fashionable as Carmel in California or Provincetown on Cape Cod.

Key West

The word "key" comes from the Spanish *cayo,* meaning a small island. It is possible that Key West was named *Cayo Oesto* by Ponce de León. But for many years it was called *Cayo Hueso*, Bone Island, perhaps because Indian battles in the 18th century left the island littered with them. Pirates and wreckers were the main inhabitants until the U.S. Navy came to plant the flag in 1822. But for all its violent past, Key West is one of the friendliest towns in Florida.

Four hours drive from Miami, the tiny subtropical island is actually nearer to Havana. Its population comprises retired military people, Cuban exiles, health-food buffs, hayfever sufferers who find the pure air here a boon, black and white descendants of the original "conchs" who came from the Bahamas, writers, painters, and a large gay community. Now they all claim to be conchs (pronounced "konks'), after the big pink mollusks which cling to the underwater rocks.

You approach the island via the newer, commercial quarter. Follow the road to the old town, past an odd group of hotels and motels, often with heated pools under tropical palms. (In

season, you'll find Key West accommodation some of the most expensive in the United States.) In **Duval Street**, lined with shops selling arts and crafts, souvenirs, T-shirts, and trash, **Sloppy Joe's** is one of the noisiest of several bars. (The place that used to have that name — Ernest Hemingway's old haunt — is round the corner in Greene Street.)

Duval Street ends at **Old Mallory Square**, scene of a nightly free show. Towards sunset, a crowd gathers on this stone quay to be entertained by musicians, jugglers, fire-eaters, and eccentrics.

Key West, the rainbow's end.

Close by Mallory Square stands the terminal of the Conch Tour Train, a mock railway engine pulling rubber-wheeled buggies on a 23-km (14-mile) trip past the island's sights. The Old Town Trolley company competes with it, and trishaws carry sightseers on shorter trips.

The **Ernest Hemingway House** (907 Whitehead Street), set in a tropical garden, was owned by the author for 30 years, although he lived here on and off for only about ten of them. But some of his most famous books, including *For Whom the Bell Tolls* and *A Farewell to Arms*, were at least partly written in Key West. A climb up the lighthouse opposite is worth it for the view.

The famous painter and naturalist John James Audubon came to Key West in 1832 to paint the birds of the Florida Keys. The so-called **Audubon House** has some good English furniture, but only a tenuous connection with the man himself. It's a bit disillusioning to learn that the great naturalist was as fond of shooting birds as he was of painting them.

On Front Street, the **Mel Fisher Museum** displays finds from the *Nuestra Señora de Atocha*, one of eight Spanish galleons wrecked in a hurricane off this coast in 1622. After years of searching, Fisher found the treasure, valued at hundreds of millions of dollars, in 1985.

Stroll through the Truman Annex, an attractive redevelopment of former naval housing, to see the immaculately restored **Truman Little White House**, favourite retreat of President Harry S. Truman in the forties and fifties. Nearby in a small state park, there's not much left of Fort Zachary Taylor, but the beach is one of the best in the area. The intense sunshine here can be a problem, so take precautions against overexposure even walking the city streets. Fortunately, Smathers Beach towards the airport has the odd palm tree or two for shade. The **coral reef** offshore breaks the waves, creating a haven for snorkellers.

THE GULF COAST

Until fairly recently, the Gulf Coast was a well-kept secret, one which European vacationers have only just begun to discover. The warm, calm waters and gently-sloping white sands are perfect for children, and there are plenty of diversions away from the beaches. The rapidly developing towns from Naples to St. Petersburg gleam in the sun, and business parks, shopping centres, and residential developments are spreading inland. Old fishing towns are being gradually eclipsed by new construction.

Quiet seclusion on one of the many islands off the west coast of Central Florida.

Much of the coastline is protected by long offshore sand-bars, which means crossing salt lagoons, by causeway or boat, to find the beach. From Marco Island near the Everglades up to Tampa Bay, 290 km (180 miles) of inlets, lakes, peninsulas, and islands make for a sailing and fishing paradise.

The elegant town of **Naples** has a fishing pier and a famous shell beach, with collectors out early in the morning to see what the tide has left behind. The Village on Venetian Bay shows how attractive a shopping mall can be, and for a view of the most luxurious waterfront homes, take a dinner cruise on a stern-wheeler around the maze of inlets.

The **Teddy Bear Museum** (2511 Pine Ridge Road) is more like a vast shop, with a few historic and collector's items. The **Collier County Museum** (Tel. 941-774-8476), located off the Tamiami Trail at the Collier County Government Center, has two hectares (five acres) devoted to local history, including a large garden of native Florida flora, a Seminole Village, and an archaeological laboratory. At the junction of Fleischmann Boulevard and U.S. 41, **Jungle Larry's Zoological Park** features big-game animals and wild birds in a tropical garden.

If you'd prefer to see creatures in the wild, follow road 846 to **Corkscrew Swamp**. The National Audubon Society has preserved a sanctuary of 4,400 hectares (11,000 acres) of wilderness here. Almost 3 km (2 miles) of boardwalks pass through the great bald cypress trees.

Fort Myers

Just south of downtown Fort Myers you can visit the **Edison Winter Home** (2350 McGregor Boulevard). The inventive genius who gave the world the light bulb, the phonograph, the stock ticker, and much more, Thomas Alva Edison (1847–1931) moved here for his health in 1886. He built a laboratory and developed the garden of exotic plants and trees in his search for new materials. The huge banyan tree was once a seedling, a gift from Harvey Firestone, founder of the tire company. The tour takes in Edison's laboratory, a collection of old cars and phonographs, and his study filled with personal effects. The great inventor's friend Henry Ford built a house right next door — you can visit that, too, though it's not of such compelling interest.

The **Shell Factory,** 6.5 km (4 miles) north of Fort Myers, has a vast collection, but it's primarily a gift shop. In the same area you can tour a citrus packing and juice extraction plant, or head inland for an interesting visit to the **ECHO project**, off Durrance Road northeast of Fort Myers. Here, in a programme to help combat world hunger, plants are tested under all sorts of conditions, and the seeds of successful varieties are sent off to developing countries.

In the same area, the **Babcock Wilderness Adventure** (off State Road 31) takes you on a ride through swamp and forest, with stops to look at the wildlife. Alligators lying across the historic trails will make you appreciate the conditions the early pioneers had to contend with. You need to telephone for reservations; the number to call is (941) 489-3911.

Offshore Retreats

Only specks on the Florida map, the string of islands that stretch like a fishhook from the mouth of the Caloosahatchee River across Charlotte Harbour are beloved and fiercely protected by their residents. **Sanibel**, the southernmost, is famous for its seashells and for the J.N. Darling National Wildlife Refuge. It's also well known for its traffic jams in high season, although you can't see much from a car and there are few places to stop. To appreciate this area and its wildlife you really need to take to the water. Tiny **Captiva** island is linked to Sanibel by a causeway, but so far North Captiva and Cayo Costa can only be reached by boat. **Boca Grande** (accessible by toll bridge via Englewood) has long been a winter hideaway for rich northerners.

North on the mainland, **Venice** has some fine public beaches. It is also the winter headquarters of the Ringling Brothers Barnum and Bailey **Circus World**, since they relocated from Sarasota.

Sarasota

This self-styled cultural capital of Florida is a favourite with visitors. The locals insist it's queen of the coast, with its own orchestra and winter seasons of ballet, opera, and theatre.

Near the centre, the **Van Wezel Performing Arts Hall** is a landmark. Completed in 1970 and dubbed the "purple people-seater," it rises by the Bay like a dramatic lavender shell. Downtown on Main Street, look for the biggest publishers' remainders bookshop outside New York City.

Sarasota's **Jungle Garden** is another of Florida's beautiful botanical gardens, stocked with a few jungle animals, and the **Selby Gardens** on the bay front have thousands of orchids and water lilies shaded by banyan trees and bamboo.

Across Ringling Causeway off U.S. 41, Sarasota's prettiest shopping and restaurant centre, **St. Armand's Circle**, is on the way to Lido Key and Beach. The next barrier island to the south, **Siesta Key** claims the whitest sand in the world and has the scientific data to prove it. Suitably wetted, it's superb for castle-building, too. Low tide brings out the shell seekers, stooping and scraping.

A replica of Michelangelo's statue of David in the courtyard of the Ringling Museum.

John and Mable Ringling of circus fame established their **estate** just north of Sarasota in the early 1920s. Within just a few years the couple had built a Venetian-style palazzo and a museum filled with hundreds of works of art that reflected their passion for the Italian Renaissance and Baroque.

The **Ringling Museum** has several of the Rubens cartoons for the *Triumph of the Eucharist* cycle (the other two extant are in the Louvre in Paris). Hals, Cranach, and Veronese are also represented in this superbly arranged collection of 14th- to 19th-century paintings. Don't miss the less-publicized paintings by Joseph Wright of Derby, Rosa Bonheur, and Burne-Jones (the extraordinary *The Sirens*). Near the museum is the **Asolo Theater**, a Rococo gem brought stone by stone from Asolo, northwest of Venice, Italy, and reassembled here in the early 1950s.

Ca' d'Zan ("John's House" in Venetian patois) has been called grandiose but if the Ringlings wanted a house in Venetian palace style, why not? It's undeniably impressive, on the shores of the bay. The crystal chandelier came from New York's Waldorf-Astoria Hotel.

The Museum of the Circus in the grounds, with its gilt circus wagons and old posters, was an afterthought on the part of the state of Florida, to which Ringling left his estate and collections. A huge range of old cars and 2,000 mechanical musical instruments — player pianos, fairground organs, musical boxes, and phonographs — can be seen at **Bellm's Cars and Music of Yesterday**, just across U.S. 41. East of Sarasota on Route 72, you can bike, drive, or take a boat trip through the **Myakka River State Park,** or hike along its 37 miles (60 km) of nature trails.

Pelicans are as common as pigeons on the Florida coast.

St. Petersburg

Farther up the coast, the impressive Sunshine Skyway toll bridge soars high over the mouth of Tampa Bay. On the north side, St. Petersburg is a quiet, sprawling city, where motel and restaurant prices are reasonable. Americans think of "St. Pete" as full of retired people, but in recent years a lot of businesses have moved here and the downtown area is in the throes of renewal. The strange-looking inverted pyramid apparently floating in the water is **Pier Place**, a complex of shops with a food court and a restaurant on top. The pier is the starting point for fishing trips and pleasure cruises.

A few blocks away on 4th Street, the **Sunken Gardens** are a tropical riot of colour, with wildlife and bird life amid the bougainvillaea and, if you like, "the world's largest gift shop." The **Salvador Dali Museum** (1000 3rd Street South) was donated to the city by two friends of Dali from Cleveland, Ohio. Opened in 1982, this huge accumulation of works by the Spanish surrealist includes paintings, sculptures, and graphics. If you find so much Dali a touch indigestible, there's an antidote waiting at the **Fine Arts Museum** on the street leading to the pier. Eclectic and accessible, with works by Renoir and Cézanne and American painters Georgia O'Keeffe, Whistler, and Grandma Moses, this collection is a delight.

Pinellas Suncoast

St. Petersburg faces the bay, but several miles away on the Gulf Coast **St. Petersburg Beach** is the start of a 32-km (20-mile) string of barrier islands stretching north to **Clearwater Beach,** and sometimes known collectively as the Pinellas Suncoast. Reached by four causeways, the strip is builtup from end to end with hotels, motels, apartment blocks, fast-food outlets, and restaurants. But don't be put off: the gently-sloping sandy beach is superb, up to 183 metres (200 yards)

The sponge-diving industry of Tarpon Springs survives to this day.

wide, with occasional piers for fishing. The sunsets are legendary, blending crimson and purple velvet.

At John's Pass, the sea separates Madeira and Treasure Island, and a bridge links them. The Village and Boardwalk here are a complex of restaurants, bars, and shops.

North of Clearwater, **Tarpon Springs** became the home of the sponge industry when Greek divers were brought here at the beginning of the 20th century. Despite diseases and competition from synthetic sponges, it's still going, though shrimp-fishing is much more important now. At **Spongeorama** you can learn about the history of sponge-diving and visit various exhibits about the marine creature whose skeleton ends up in your bath.

Forty-eight km (30 miles) up the coast, the **Weeki Wachee** theme park features birds-of-prey shows and water slides, but the main attraction is an improbable underwater ballet, *The Little Mermaid*. Maidens with flowing hair and fishtails hold their breath, smile bravely, and perform acrobatics.

Tampa

The big city of the Gulf Coast is still quite compact, but growing fast, upwards in the centre and outwards away from the bay. Major restoration is in progress at **Ybor City**, where there were once 200 cigar factories employing thousands of Cuban workers, displaced from their homeland in the 19th century. The Great Depression of the 1930s dealt the industry a near-fatal blow.

The area along 7th and 8th Avenues between 13th and 22nd streets has remained in a time warp. Now, among the Cuban snack bars and little businesses, souvenir shops, antiques shops, and fancier restaurants have sprung up.

Busch Gardens

In a huge park northeast of Tampa, brewing giant Anheuser-Busch has piled on the attractions as if trying to outdo all its rivals. "The Dark Continent" is the overall theme and the buildings are just like those of southern Morocco. Collect a map at the entrance: the layout of the park is confusing.

The open plains of the **Serengeti** with their big game animals and herds of grazing zebras and antelopes can be viewed from cable cars, a monorail, or an old-fashioned train. Try all three. You can go white-water rafting on the Congo River or scream down a waterfall. There's an ice show and a thrilling simulator ride, **Questor**, supposedly an eccentric British professor's universal travelling machine. The Python and Scorpion **roller coasters** turn you upside-down at breakneck speed, and a giant swingboat, **The Phoenix**, does the same thing very slowly.

You are invited to tour the on-site brewery and to sample the beers at Hospitality House if you are 21 years of age or over. You can easily take a full day to see Busch Gardens and get value for your money.

Nearby **Adventure Island** water park (same owners) has waterfalls, waterslides, and waves. It closes in winter.

WHAT TO DO

SPORTS

With a winter like other people's summers and seas as tempting as a tropical lagoon, Florida will have you out and playing before you can get your bags unpacked.

Golf and tennis practically have the status of religions here. The waters are ideal for sailing, canoeing, and fishing. You can go hiking, riding, and hunting (here it means shooting). Spectator sports at various times of year include football, baseball, basketball, and even polo. You can watch and bet on greyhounds and horses and the local speciality, jai alai, a super-fast version of squash played with a hybrid of a hockey stick and a sling.

Sports cars, grand prix cars, and stock cars race the famous tracks at Daytona and Sebring and the streets of Miami. Then there's the most popular outdoor activity of all — hitting the beach and occasionally cooling off in the sea.

Watersports

Practically everyone's first idea is to get on, into, or under the water. Whether you prefer windsurfing, scuba diving, waterskiing, or just plain swimming, Florida's beaches and sheltered inland waterways have room enough for everybody.

Chances for **scuba diving** exist along the Atlantic coast, but the best area is around the Florida Keys, including more than 32 km (20 miles) of coral reef in John Pennekamp State Park (see page 69). You'll need a certified diver's card or else take classes when you arrive; details can be obtained from any diving shop.

Snorkelling amid the brilliant fish is exhilarating, too. Everyone is urged not even to touch the coral, and it's illegal to take any of it. You can hire all the necessary equipment; shop around for the best prices.

Big waves for **surfing** are mainly restricted to the Atlantic coast — Cocoa Beach and Melbourne Beach are favourites. Waters protected by Florida's many barrier islands or the generally calmer seas of the Gulf Coast are ideal for **water-skiing** or **windsurfing**.

With a coastline this long, **beaches** are countless — and often almost endless (Daytona's, for instance, runs for 37 km/23 miles), though access may be restricted by private property. If the crowd is too dense for you in one spot, a short walk will earn you some solitude — most people don't stray far from their cars.

There's an occasional problem with jellyfish, including the stinging Portuguese man-of-war, or accumulations of weed, and Atlantic storms can sometimes wash away a stretch of sand.

Popular beaches usually have lifeguards, especially at weekends. Many have barbecue facilities, too, but alcohol, glass containers, and pets are frequently banned.

Beware of the power of the sun, especially if you are snorkelling: your back can feel cool and still burn quite badly, unless you've applied waterproof sunblock.

The spectacular coral reef can be seen during a scuba diving adventure.

Boating and Sailing No holiday in Florida would be complete without at least one outing on the water. Power-boats, sailboats, and canoes in profusion are available for hire. You can sail nearly everywhere. Some of the best power-boating is from Everglades City among the Ten Thousand Islands and down south in Florida Bay. Navigational charts are available at marinas and map dealers.

Airboat rides are a noisy but exciting way of skimming shallows and swamps, and **glass-bottom boats** let you see the coral reefs without getting wet.

There are also some 35 official **canoeing** trails through the Everglades and on the rivers flowing from central Florida's springs and lakes. The state's Department of Natural Resources publishes a free guide (3900 Commonwealth Boulevard, Tallahassee, FL 32399-3000). To hire canoes, look in the *Yellow Pages* under Boat Dealers, or ask at the local chamber of commerce.

Fishing Hundreds of different species of fish inhabit the rivers, creeks, and seas. You can hire rods and reels, or, if you're an enthusiast, this is a good place to buy equipment. Bait shops at the docks and fishing piers will give you free advice on what to fish for. Often your biggest problem will

Coconut Grove Harbour.

*Fishing in Florida is a favourite pastime
and can bring the greatest catches.*

be competition from pelicans, who hang about in the hopes of stealing away with some of your catch. In the process they may get hooked themselves: if it happens, release them with extreme care. (Get help if you can.)

Marinas everywhere are crowded with expensive deep-sea fishing boats for hire — they come complete with a knowledgeable captain. Beyond that the only thing you'll need is plenty of patience. Some boats go for the more certain mackerel and amberjack, but you can try for the big ones — marlin and shark, or the exciting if inedible tarpon which can weigh from 30 to 45 kg (60 to 100 lbs).

A number of resorts have a branch of FISH (Florida Inland Sportsfishing Hosts), dedicated to making you a regular visitor. They publish brochures mapping the waters, and listing accommodations, campgrounds, and fishing regulations. Okeechobee is good for lake fishing, and big bass are also found in the rivers or in Lake George. Canals are well stocked and sometimes turn up saltwater fish such as tarpon or snook.

For information on boating and fishing, write to the Department of Natural Resources, 3900 Commonwealth Boule-

Spend a day golfing on one of the many challenging and sprawling green courses.

vard, Tallahassee, FL 32399-3000. You'll need a visitor's licence if you are over 16 and plan to do any fishing, whether saltwater or freshwater. These are available at marinas and tackle shops.

Hiking. Most people stick to walking or jogging along the beaches, but there are plenty of marked trails in the national forests and state parks. Only members of the Florida Trail Association may use trails across private property. Membership isn't expensive. Write to: Florida Trail Association Inc, P.O. Box 13708, Gainesville, Florida, FL 32604.

Golf. There are over 1,000 golf courses in the state of Florida – over 40 courses in Greater Miami alone, plus a heavy concentration up the Gold Coast, the Gulf Coast, and in the centre and the north of Florida. Some holiday companies offer packages including green fees, but even the regular prices are reasonable, especially if you start after 3:00 P.M. If you haven't brought your equipment, clubs and even shoes are for rent at some courses, and Florida abounds with golf shops. You may be required to hire and use a ride-on buggy (and to heed warnings not to run over any alligators). Local chambers of commerce will supply lists of courses.

Resort courses have plenty of staff who need tipping, they won't let you carry your clubs at all. Avoid playing at mid-day in summer. Even the usually ubiquitous drinks carts can't make it pleasurable. Rates are lower in summer when the crowds have gone.

Tennis. Many larger hotels have courts; some resorts have teaching facilities and organize tournaments. Miami Beach has nearly 50 courts in two separate tennis centres. In Orlando you can book the clay courts of Orlando Tennis Club or the asphalt ones at the public club in Winter Park. Walt Disney World's Contemporary Resort has a tennis clinic with video equipment, practice lanes, and automatic ball machines. Anywhere in Florida you won't be far from a tennis club, but in summer it's best to play in the early morning or late after-noon, avoiding the combination of hot sun and humidity.

Hunting. Most tourists on a two-week jaunt to Florida don't come for the hunting scene. Nevertheless, parts of northern Florida offer the best wild turkey shooting; rabbit, fox, and raccoon can be shot almost everywhere, and deer in some wilder districts. Licenses are necessary. Contact the Game and Freshwater Fish Commission for further details.

Spectator Sports. The climate makes the state ideal for northern **baseball** teams to keep fit during the winter. The Boston Red Sox, Baltimore Orioles, and many others play spring training games in several Florida cities. The state has also welcomed a recent influx of professional sports teams. Florida now boasts a baseball team, the world-champion Marlins; an ice hockey team, the Panthers; and pro basket-ball's The Miami Heat.

In professional **football**, Miami has its famous Dol-phins, who play at Pro Player Stadium (home of the Mar-lins), and Tampa Bay is the base of the Buccaneers. Miami's huge **Orange Bowl** is home to the University of

Miami Hurricanes and on 1 January each year the two top college teams meet in the Orange Bowl Classic.

Florida hosts some major **tennis** tournaments, notably the Lipton International on Key Biscayne in March.

As for professional **golf**, the Doral-Ryder PGA Open is held in Miami every February or March, followed by the Honda Classic.

Buy your goggles and snorkels in the middle of the night at Ton Jon Surf Shop in Cocoa Beach.

Horse racing takes place at Miami's Hialeah Park (short winter season), Calder Race Course just north of Miami, Gulfstream Park at Hallandale, Florida Downs at Tampa (January to mid-March), and Gator Down, Pompano, which also has harness racing. (See the local press for details.) **Greyhound racing** venues include Daytona, Hollywood, Key West, Miami, Orlando, and Tampa. If you prefer a more rarefied entertainment, **polo** is a popular winter sport at Boca Raton.

Most intriguing to a visitor is the action-packed Basque game of **jai alai** (pronounced "high ligh"). You'll see it played at night in season at the Miami Fronton (3500 NW 37th Avenue), and at Dania, Daytona, and Tampa. Tickets are cheap, because the idea is to get you in to bet on the *parimutuel* (tote) system, which also runs the gambling at the dog and horse races.

Finally, **cars** and **motorbikes** race at Daytona International Speedway. In February, thousands gather for the famous Daytona 500, and the central Florida town of Sebring stages its 12-hour international sports car race every March. Miami's Grand Prix in Monaco-style uses city streets, including Biscayne Boulevard.

SHOPPING

America's marketing wizards can come up with bargains in every sort of product, as well as a vast choice. Check the prices the discount stores advertise in weekend editions of the local newspapers. If you're attracted by electronics don't forget that American equipment runs on 110 volts, so make sure that what you buy can be adapted to your home voltage.

Prices vary enormously from store to store. A swimsuit bought at a sea-front hotel boutique may be four times the cost of an identical one in a department store 200 yards away. It pays to shop around.

Even better bargains are found at the sales which most stores hold several times a year, usually after Christmas, the 4th of July, and other holidays. A sales tax of around 6.5 percent is added to the ticket price of all purchases.

When and Where to Shop

Hours vary: suburban malls are open 7 days a week, 10:00 A.M. to 9:00 P.M., while shops in city centres are generally open only until around 5:30 P.M., closing on Sundays. Large chain stores close only for national holidays — and not all of them.

In addition to the shopping centres, supermarkets, speciality shops, discount, and chain stores, Florida has a style of shopping found only in the world's prosperous places: prestige malls. The very buildings reflect the wares within. Featuring tropical landscaping, modern sculpture, and fountains, they are often innovatively designed by creative architects. Inside, the best of American designer boutiques, antiques and jewellery shops alternate with branches of famous European fashion houses. Even if the prices are out of your league, there's nothing to stop you from window shopping.

What to Buy

Florida keeps its eyes on Europe, New York, and California, and responds to fashion with the latest in **leisurewear**, swimsuits, robes, and shoes.

"Western stores" sell leather goods and **cowboy clothes**. This is a cattle state, so they actually supply real cowboys and ranchers, not just tourists, though the merchandise these days is not always made in the United States. A well-fitting pair of cowboy boots will last for years. You can also get fringed Indian jackets, jeans, silver buckles, leather hats and gloves, and tooled leather handbags and wallets.

Some stores stock **Indian crafts** from all over America, including fine woven blankets, ponchos, wall hangings, and skirts. The local Seminoles specialize in patchwork children's clothing. You can bargain for semi-precious jewellery, often turquoise stones set in silverwork, and artistic pottery. The prices may seem a bit high — they've risen considerably in recent years.

It might seem strange to come here and buy Oriental and Asian goods, but the import stores have bargains in woven raffia, wood, leather, and wicker furniture and rugs.

America is the home of gadgets and electronic marvels, from toys to laptop computers — many of them imported, but often you'll find them cheaper here. **Sports** enthusiasts should check out the equipment on sale, especially for golf, tennis, and fishing.

And finally, you can send back a box of Florida sunshine. The larger roadside stands will pack their own tangerines, oranges, grapefruits, or a mixture and ship it home for you.

ENTERTAINMENT

In downtown **Miami,** concentrated in Little Havana, the dominant note is Cuban, the exiles showing what, for better or worse, the old country was like before the revolution. Supper-clubs and *discotecas* raise the temperature with the latest merengue, salsa, and cumbia sounds. "Anglos" may need to take some lessons before going public on the dance floor in a lambada. For them, the choice widens in **Miami Beach**, especially along trendy Ocean Drive and Washington Avenue in South Beach, where bars and restaurants feature live jazz and clubs come and go with bewildering speed. Rock, reggae, '60s revival, gay clubs, British and Irish pubs — any excuse for drinking and dancing will do.

The scene is just as varied in **Coconut Grove**. On Friday and Saturday nights you'll think everyone in Miami has come here to cruise the streets and pack the bars. Music blares from cars and cafés until the small hours, and street performers entertain the crowd. If you prefer something quieter, Miami and the Beach also have dozens of piano-bars. Some agencies organize tours of the nightclubs in a package that includes cocktails at one and dinner at another, sometimes followed by a floor show.

Colourful cloth weavings produced by local Seminole Indians.

Orlando has cashed in on the theme-park traffic with nightclubs, western saloons, and cancan dancers on the bar, in and around downtown Church Street

Station. Walt Disney World tries to keep its guests on site for the evenings with all-American music — Dixieland, folk, Country and Western, disco, and heavy metal — in the bars and dance halls of Pleasure Island. Disney's hotels have shows of their own, from Tahitian hula dancing at the Polynesian Resort to Broadway-type musical spectacles at the Contemporary Resort.

Other themed dinner-show packages in the Orlando area include "Arabian Nights" (with 60 horses), "Fort Liberty" (Wild West), "King Henry's Feast," and "Medieval Times." You'll be elbow to elbow and the humour is unsubtle, but they're competitively priced, well-organized, and fun.

Theatre, Concerts, Opera, and Ballet

Broadway sends touring shows to Miami Beach's Jackie Gleason Theater, the Coconut Grove Playhouse, and to Palm Beach, Fort Lauderdale, and Sarasota. That specially American institution, the dinner-theatre, where you can get a meal and a play, is available at Fort Lauderdale and Tampa.

Classical and rock concerts take place year-round in Miami at the Gusman Center for the Performing Arts and the Convention Center across from Du Pont Plaza. Dade Country Auditorium (2901 West Flagler Street) is the venue for the winter seasons of Greater Miami Opera and the Miami City Ballet.

Sarasota declares itself to be the cultural capital of the state and backs up the claim with concerts, ballet, opera, and theatre performances at the Van Wezel Hall and at the Ringling Museum's Asolo Center.

Key West specializes in casual live music in its bars and cafés. The Tennessee Williams Playhouse, as its name might suggest, offers drama a little more demanding than the musical comedies up the coast.

CALENDAR OF EVENTS

There are many special events held in Florida. A few are listed here: buy a copy of the *What's On* magazine for more details.

January
- *Greek Festival* (Tarpon Springs)
- *Art Deco Weekend* (Miami Beach)
- *Three Kings Parade* (Miami's Little Havana). Latin spectacle, with bands, floats, marching, and dancing.

February
- *Silver Spurs Rodeo* (Kissimmee). A semi-annual fair with calf-roping, steer-wrestling, and other cowboy feats.
- *Old Island Days* (Key West). Conch-blowing contest, parades, and other events commemorate the early history of the island.
- *Big Orange Music Festival* (Miami). Dade county-wide celebration, featuring every type of music from classical to rock.
- *Miami International Film Festival*
- *Kissimmee Valley Livestock Show Fair*

March/April
- *Easter Sunrise Service* (Cypress Gardens). A service held at dawn on Easter Sunday.

April
- *Miami Grand Prix*
- *JazzFest Kissimmee*

July
- *Silver Spurs Rodeo* (Kissimmee). February event repeated.
- *All-American Water Ski Championship* (Cypress Gardens). The pros contend in Florida's waterskiing capital.

September
- *Anniversary of the Founding of St. Augustine*
- *Osceola Art Festival*

October
- *Hispanic Heritage Week Gala* (Miami)

December/January
- *Orange Bowl Festival* (Miami). Highlight is the Orange Bowl Parade on New Year's Eve.

EATING OUT

Florida is a veritable cornucopia of citrus fruit, vegetables, salad crops, beef, fish, and shellfish. Anything missing is simply shipped in.

When to Eat

You'll find some places are even open round the clock. Breakfast is served from 6:00 or 7:00 to 11:00 A.M., lunch from about 11:30 A.M. to 1:30 P.M. and dinner from 5:00 or 6:00 until 9:00 or 10:00 P.M. Brunch is featured on Sundays between 11:00 A.M. and 3:00 P.M. Some restaurants offer an "early-bird special," dinner at a lower price if you order before 5:00 or 6:00 P.M.

Where to Eat

Fierce competition has resulted in amazing bargains at the lower end of the price range — fast-food, ethnic and "family" restaurants and the all-you-can-eat buffets are usually very good value. A more elegant meal will cost from twice to ten times as much — sometimes worth the extra expense. Seek local advice — hotel staff are often experts and free with their opinions. (See also the RESTAURANTS section on p. 139.)

Delicatessen restaurants specialize in gargantuan sandwiches of corned beef, smoked turkey, roast beef, and many other fillings. Cream cheese and lox (smoked salmon) on a bagel (a kind of firm bread roll) ranks high among deli specialities, along with chopped liver and pastrami.

Takeaways. As well as the fast-food outlets, the delicatessen or cold meat counters in the better supermarkets are a great place to pick up a **picnic.**

Breakfast. Continental comprises juice, coffee, and toast or a sweet pastry. Eggs appear on every menu, along with bacon, grits, and sausages, french toast, waffles, and pancakes.European visitors may find American coffee rather weak, although refills are offered as a matter of course. If you crave more flavour, find a Cuban snack bar or coffee stall and drink little cups of aromatic *café cubano. Buche* is the strong black espresso variety.

Soups. You can almost make a meal of thick and filling seafood bisque, navy bean, or Cuban black bean soup. Conch chowder, available on the Keys, combines milk, potatoes, vegetables, spices, and chopped conch, a type of shellfish.

Salads. Many restaurants offer self-service salad bars. Otherwise, a salad frequently comes with the main course Chef's salad is a meal in itself, made with lettuce, cheese, ham, turkey, or other cold meats.

Seafood. Florida's fish and shellfish include red snapper, yellowtail, grouper, jumbo shrimp, stone crab, and crawfish ("Florida lobster"). Don't be afraid to order dolphin, not the friendly mammal but a tasty fish. A lot of

---

Spoiled for Choice

Your eating options are as varied as the strands that make up the population — and then some. Italian, Spanish, Mexican, Chinese, Thai, Vietnamese, Japanese, Greek, French — even British pubs serving fish and chips. Cuban cooking prevails in much of Miami, with Haitian and other Caribbean cuisines making an impact, and the Jewish community has brought the best of delicatessen food from New York.

And remember, this is part of the South so you'll be offered grits (like unsweetened semolina) and gumbo (spicy stew with okra). In northern Florida you'll see hog jowls and collard greens in the supermarkets and boiled peanuts on the roadside stalls — a gastronomic trip for the adventurous!

restaurants avoid confusion by using the Hawaiian name "mahi mahi." Nothing compares with the flavour of freshly caught broiled (grilled) fish, served with a simple lemon and butter sauce. In the cheapest places it's unlikely to be fresh from the sea, but will probably have been frozen. There's a tendency to "bread" everything, so specify if you don't want that. Shrimps come broiled, fried, or steamed — sometimes in beer.

Stone crabs, a seasonal delicacy, have a devoted following. Diners don bibs to eat the meat, extracting it from the claws with the aid of a nutcracker and dipping it into a lemon and butter or mustard and mayonnaise sauce.

You'll often see Raw Bars advertised. They usually serve oysters — often the only raw seafood actually on offer. If the names confuse you, order a combination seafood platter, served hot or cold. Meat lovers can have their steak and eat seafood too — "Surf and Turf" is a steak and seafood platter.

You may get a taste for conch fritters (deep-fried pieces of the shellfish), especially on the Keys. Chefs inland favour catfish, a freshwater variety that is fried and served with hush puppies (not shoes, but fried cornmeal balls).

Meats. Steaks, roast beef and southern fried chicken dominate. Most Cuban restaurants offer *picadillo* (marinated ground beef mixed with olives, green peppers, garlic, onions, and tomato sauce) and *arroz con pollo* (chicken and rice). A popular Mexican dish is an *enchilada*, a tortilla (cornmeal pancake) stuffed with a meat filling and baked with sauce.

Gourmet cuisine in a greenhouse atmosphere.

Vegetables. Except at some health-food and ethnic restaurants, cooked vegetables are not served in great variety. A notable exception is fresh corn on the cob. Yams, candied and baked, are a legacy of the Old South, and the starchy root yuca features on some Cuban menus.

Desserts. Sweet and creamy Key lime pie turns up everywhere in Florida, but especially on the Keys. Boston cream pie is a sponge cake filled with custard and topped with rich chocolate. Cheesecake reigns supreme in half a dozen varieties (strawberry, blueberry, pineapple — and, of course, Key lime).

Drinks. Fresh fruit juices are excellent. The big brand name soft drinks are everywhere, iced water is almost universal and iced tea is an American speciality.

Cold beer is comparable to European lager, but standard U.S. brands taste sweeter. Many foreign beers are either imported or manufactured under license. "Light" (or "Lite") doesn't mean low alcohol here, just lower in calories.

House wines come by the bottle, carafe, or glass. If you order from the list, the French and Italian wines are generally no better than the Californian at similar prices. Some restaurants have no license to sell wine, but won't mind if you bring your own bottle. The waiter will open it and provide glasses for a small charge.

Cocktails are served by the glass or, more economically, by the pitcher. The ever-popular piña colada combines rum, pineapple juice, and coconut milk. Daiquiris are made with rum and an assortment of fruit juices — peach, strawberry, or banana, for example. Mimosa is champagne and orange juice and a margarita is a mixture of fresh lime juice, tequila, and ice.

A warning: liquor laws are strictly enforced. You can buy beer and wine in many grocery stores, but spirits are sold only in liquor stores. Cans and bottles of beer, wine, or spirits must not be displayed in public places, but be kept in bags at all times. Alcohol is prohibited on many beaches, and no one under 21 years of age is permitted to buy alcohol. You may be asked for "ID," an identification document showing your date of birth.

Florida Gold

The state's vast citrus groves make it the world's biggest producer of many varieties. Growers large and small have assortments packed ready to send off as soon as an order is received.

Here are some of the most popular varieties:

Navel oranges: Easy to peel, thin-skinned and juicy, navels are in season in November.

Temple oranges: Richer in flavour than navels, temples peel like a tangerine — and are virtually seedless.

Valencia oranges: Late-ripeners, Valencias appear at the fruit stands from March to May. They're particularly tasty in fruit salads.

Tangerines: Robinson tangerines ripen in October and November. In December and January you'll find the Dancy variety; in March, the extra-sweet Honey tangerines.

Tangelos: A Florida hybrid, tangelos combine the easy-eating qualities of the tangerine with the flavour of a sweet grapefruit.

Grapefruit: From the Indian River district, Marsh Whites have a nobler, austere acidity; Ruby Reds are sweeter.

Pomelos: Like a bigger, coarser, sweeter grapefruit.

Kumquats: Farmers often give away these little treats, which look like miniature, oval oranges. You eat the whole thing, sweet rind and all. Ask for some when you buy fruit.

Limes: Put an aromatic slice of green lime in your gin and tonic and you'll never go back to lemon.

INDEX

HANDY TRAVEL TIPS

An A–Z Summary of Practical Information

A

ACCOMMODATION. (*See also* HOTELS AND CAMPING *section.*)

Florida offers a huge variety of accommodation in every price range. However, in high season reservations may be hard to come by, especially at Walt Disney World and in popular beach resorts. Book well in advance, even a year may not be too much for the Christmas and Easter holidays.

American hotels and motels usually charge by the room, not the number of occupants, but hard-sell advertising may quote a per person rate. State and sometimes local taxes are added to the bill (see page 117). Most rooms have two double beds, private bathroom (a shower in budget motels), and colour TV. There may be a refrigerator and cooking facilities.

Efficiencies are small apartments with kitchenette or separate kitchen and dining area. Facilities include dishes, pans, and cutlery. In recent years, tour operators have been offering more and more self-catering villas and apartments.

In coastal areas, the farther from the beach you go, the lower the rates should be. Rooms facing a pool or garden are often two-thirds the price of rooms with an ocean view.

High season in Florida is from 15 December to March or April (including Easter). Quietest times are in May and June and between September and November, when prices are generally lower. Some resort hotels offer special rates to guests who take meals on the premises: American Plan includes three meals a day and the Modified American Plan includes breakfast and either lunch or dinner.

Larger hotels employ a concierge/bell captain who can arrange tours, call a cab, or hire a car for you, but you may be able to economize by making your own arrangements.

AIRPORTS

Miami International Airport (MIA) is a crowded and confusing place, just west of the city centre. Served by more than 60 airlines, it's one of the world's busiest airports, with two terminals connected by an automated "peoplemover." The main terminal, divided into concourses (or zones), has two floors, the lower level for arrivals and baggage claim and the upper for departures and ticketing. Here you'll find bars, fast-food restaurants, telephones, shops, and an information desk open 24 hours a day. If you're not well supplied with dollars, change money at one of the exchange counters. It's unwise to go into town without sufficient U.S. currency.

Orlando (McCoy) International Airport (ORL or MCO) is spacious, glittering, and constantly expanding. There are two terminals, each with shops, restaurants, and exchange counters. Automatic trains shuttle people to satellite gates. No trolleys are provided, so suitcases with wheels are recommended.

At both airports, red and green customs channels are in operation and formalities are generally simple and quick.

Ground transport. From Miami International, a taxi to Miami Beach usually takes 15–25 minutes (up to an hour during rush hour). The bright blue vehicles of the Airport Region Taxi Service (ARTS) carry passengers to nearby destinations for a low flat fare. "Red Top" minibuses will take you to almost any hotel downtown or on Miami Beach for a third of the taxi fare. Cheaper still are the municipal buses, leaving every 30 to 45 minutes from the main terminal's lower level. The Tri-Rail system runs to Gold Coast resorts.

From Orlando International, taxis and shuttle minibuses operate to downtown Orlando, International Drive and Walt Disney World, and to Cocoa Beach. Some hotels run a free shuttle. A municipal bus runs to downtown Orlando.

Check-in time. Arrive at least one hour before domestic flights, and one hour and a half before international flights. (The airlines suggest two hours.) For flight information, call your airline.

Other Florida airports. Fort Lauderdale, West Palm Beach, Key West, and Tampa have their own international airports, and several other cities are served by domestic flights.

Florida

Domestic flights. Air travel is by far the quickest and most convenient way of getting round the U.S. A few of the most-travelled routes have shuttle services. Travellers from abroad can buy a Visit USA ticket, which provides discounts and sets no fixed programme. These must be bought before you arrive in the U.S. (or within 15 days of arrival).

Fares change constantly, so it is wise to consult a travel agent for the latest information about special deals.

B

BICYCLE HIRE

Popular beach resorts have shops which hire out bicycles by the hour, day, or week. They are an ideal way to get around Key West, for example, with its parking problems and short distances. There are few segregated cycle tracks (Coconut Grove is an exception). Make sure a lock is included and check on insurance against theft.

C

CAMPING

Camping in America generally involves recreational vehicles (RVs) — campers, motor homes, or caravans (trailers). If you are camping the American way, the *Rand McNally Campground and Trailer Park Guide* or the voluminous *Woodalls* list and grade campgrounds according to their facilities. (A campsite in the U.S. means the actual spot where you put your RV or tent.) The *Florida State Parks Guide,* a map of all the excellent state parks and state recreational areas with camping facilities, is available from:

> **The Florida Department of Natural Resources**
> Bureau of Education and Information
> 3900 Commonwealth Boulevard
> Tallahassee, FL 32399-3000

In each state park, your length of stay is limited to two weeks. To avoid disappointment, reserve a place in advance by telephone.

Camping beside the road — or on private land without permission — is both illegal and unsafe.

CAR HIRE

Hot competition among car hire companies ("car rental companies" in the U.S.) keeps rates relatively low, and automatic and air-conditioned cars are the norm. If you can pick up and return the car at the same place, try one of the local businesses. If you plan to drop it off in another city, it's best to reserve a car before you get to the U.S. at one of the international companies — it will be cheaper.

The well-known car hire agencies charge higher rental rates, but may include insurance costs in the price: small companies, with little or no insurance included in the rates, offer what may sound like fairly expensive insurance coverage. One way or another, you are advised to make sure you have CDW (collision damage waiver), or you will have to pay for some or all of the cost of repairs.

Many inclusive holidays and fly-drive packages promise a "free car," but you will usually have to pay Florida taxes and CDW when you collect it.

Drivers over 25 with a valid driving license can hire a car. Some agencies make exceptions for 18-year-old drivers paying with a credit card. For tourists from non-English-speaking countries, a translation of the driving license may be requested, together with the national license itself, or failing this, an International Driving Permit.

Invariably, it is more convenient to pay with a major credit card rather than cash. If you have no card, you must leave a large deposit. Sometimes cash is refused at night and on weekends. To extend your hire, inform the original office, or stop at the nearest branch office.

CHILDREN'S FLORIDA

There should be no problem keeping children happy, whether at the many and varied theme parks or on the beaches (the Gulf Coast generally has calmer water and safe, gently sloping sands). Most hotels and many motels have pools. The sun, heat, and humidity can take their toll, especially in the form of dehydration, so make sure your children get plenty to drink. American restaurants are used to accommodating all ages, but when you want to escape, large hotels can provide babysitters.

CLIMATE

Most of the year Florida weather ranges from warm to hot, but the coasts are agreeably cooled by sea breezes. The peak tourist season is winter, when temperatures and rainfall are at their lowest. You may encounter a brief spell of cool weather, but not often cold enough to interfere with swimming and sunbathing. From June to October it's hot and humid, and you can expect some rain most days, though rarely so persistent as to be troublesome.

Some tourist brochures boast that you'll never need warm clothing, even in the middle of winter, but prudence suggests otherwise. In winter, Atlantic beaches can be very windy, and there may be some rainy days and cold spells. Even in the south temperatures *can* dip to near freezing for short periods, though many winter days see temperatures in the 80s, especially in south Florida and on the Keys.

Hurricanes hardly ever happen. On average, Florida is hit only one year in seven and only between June and November, so your chance of being in the wrong place at the wrong time is minimal.

Average daytime temperatures for Miami:

Average temperatures

	J	F	M	A	M	J	J	A	S	O	N	D
°C	21	21	22	24	26	27	28	29	27	26	23	21
°F	69	70	71	74	78	81	82	84	81	78	73	70

CLOTHING

Whenever it's hot or humid, Floridians turn on the air conditioners. These can blow with arctic chill, so don't forget to take a wrap with you when shopping, dining out, or riding in air-conditioned vehicles — including city buses. Winter can bring surprisingly cold spells, so be ready for any eventuality.

In resorts, casual wear is appropriate round the clock, something light, bright, loose, and made of cotton rather than artificial fibres. Palm Beach is an exception, favouring crisp, conservative and — for men — nautical fashions. If you're likely to go swimming often, pack spare swimwear for a rapid change. Other useful items to bring include an umbrella, sunhat, and comfortable sports-type shoes for tramping round theme parks or along rocky trails.

COMPLAINTS

If you have a serious complaint about business practices and have talked with the manager of the establishment in question to no avail, you may contact the:

Agriculture Department
Consumer Services Division
The Capitol
Tallahassee, FL 32301

CRIME (*See also* EMERGENCIES.)

Buying and selling illegal drugs is a serious offence. Florida has a large force of undercover officers (plain-clothes police) who are battling to keep drugs out.

Most hotels have a safe for valuables. Never leave money, credit cards, cheque books, etc., in a hotel room, but always in the safe.

In Miami, beware of pickpockets on city buses, in queues, crowded stores, and elevators (lifts). The Miami police warn you to drive with windows up and doors locked, especially in areas with numerous traffic lights. Would-be thieves may stage fake accidents or tell you there's something wrong with your car to get you to stop. All belongings should be placed in the trunk (boot) of the car while you are driving.

An unfortunate trend in the Miami area is the increase in crimes of violence. Go out after dark in groups, not alone, and avoid carrying large amounts of cash or valuables. Leave your car with the attendant at a restaurant, nightclub, or discotheque, rather than parking it yourself on a dimly lit side street. Use normal common sense and avoid certain areas, especially Liberty City in northwest Miami. Avoid sightseeing at night in Downtown Miami, as it is easy to get lost.

CUSTOMS and ENTRY FORMALITIES

U.K. citizens and some other foreign visitors no longer require a visa to enter the U.S., and instead can obtain a visa waiver form from their travel agent or airline. Canadians need only provide evidence of their nationality. Citizens of the Republic of Ireland, Australia, New Zealand, and South Africa need a visa (but rules change, so check with your local U.S. embassy or consulate, or travel agent).

Duty-free allowance. You will be asked to complete a customs declaration form before you arrive in the U.S. The chart shows what main duty-free items you may take into the U.S. (if you are over 21) and, when returning home, into your own country.

Into:	Cigarettes		Cigars		Tobacco	Spirits		Wine
U.S.	200	or	50	or	1,350 g	1 *liter*	or	1 *liter*
Australia	200	or	250 g	or	250 g	1 *l.*	or	1 *l.*
Canada	200	and	50	and	900 g	1.1 *l.*	or	1.1 *l.*
Eire	200	or	50	or	250 g	1 l.	and	2 *l.*
N. Zealand	200	or	50	or	250 g	1.1 *l.*	and	4.5 *l.*
S. Africa	400	and	50	and	250 g	1 *l.*	and	2 *l.*
U.K.	200	or	50	or	250 g	1 *l.*	and	2 *l.*

A non-resident may claim, free of duty and taxes, articles up to $100 in value for use as gifts. Plants and foodstuffs are subject to strict control; visitors from abroad may not import fruits, vegetables, meat, or liqueur chocolates.

Arriving and departing passengers must report any money or cheques exceeding a total of $10,000.

DRIVING

Drive on the right. In Florida, you may turn right after stopping at a red light, provided there is no cross-traffic, you have given way to pedestrians, and there is no sign to the contrary. Never drive at night without headlights: it's strictly illegal. Switch on headlights also when it rains enough for wipers to be needed. Front seat belts must be worn and you must carry your driving license.

Lane discipline differs from European norms. American drivers tend to stick to one lane, making no distinction between fast or "slow" lanes except to some extent on the Interstate network. You may therefore be overtaken on either side, so don't change lanes without careful checking. In populated areas, the middle lane is generally for making left turns only.

Don't drink and drive — driving while intoxicated (DWI) may get you locked up.

Expressways (motorways). On the high-speed divided highways called expressways, driving follows certain rules. Rather than accelerate up the ramp (slip road) to join the traffic at its own speed, you hesitate at the top of the ramp and wait for an opening. A national speed limit of 55 mph (88 km/h) operates on highways, except on expressways in rural areas, where the limit is 65 mph (105 km/h). Other limits such as 45 mph (72 km/h) apply where indicated. If you keep up with the flow of traffic, you'll have no problem, but go any faster, and a patrol car may pull you over.

If you have a breakdown on an expressway, pull over on to the right-hand shoulder, tie a handkerchief to the door handle or radio aerial, raise the bonnet (hood), and wait in the car for assistance. At night, use the hazard warning lights.

Tolls. In Florida tolls are collected at turnpikes, and at many bridges and causeways. Keep a supply of coins when travelling; most toll areas provide a basket into which you drop the right change, so there's no waiting.

Petrol (gas) and services. Florida's service stations have both self-service and full-service pumps, fuel at the latter being much more expensive. They offer regular, middle, and premium grades — regular is adequate for most rental cars. In some areas it is necessary to pre-pay, especially at night. Some pumps are operated by inserting a credit card (and major international cards are accepted). Note that many stations close in the evenings and on Sundays.

Florida

Most rental cars in Florida are equipped with air conditioners; if your car is running low on fuel or overheating, turn it off — it's a strain on the engine.

Parking. Florida's famous attractions usually have large and inexpensive (rarely free) car parks. Most municipal car parks have metres; the coins required and the times of operation are always noted on them. Spaces in the streets are indicated by white lines painted on the road. Your car must point in the direction of the flow of traffic, or nose-in where angle-parking is indicated. (Florida cars don't have number plates in front.) Do not park by a fire hydrant or a kerb painted yellow or red.

Directions. Try to get help planning your route if you don't know the area you are heading for. Don't assume that if you hit the right number street, avenue, or road you can continue to your destination. It may come to a dead end or pass through undesirable places. The expressways are usually the quickest way of crossing the big cities.

Note that road numbers are generally even for east-west routes, odd for north-south.

The American Automobile Association offers assistance to members of affiliated organizations abroad. It also provides travel information for the U.S. and can arrange automobile insurance by the month for owner-drivers. Contact the AAA at 1000 AAA Drive, Heathrow, FL 32746-5063; tel. (407) 444-7000.

Road signs. Although the U.S. has begun to change over to international road signs, progress is gradual. Some of the terms used may be unfamiliar or confusing.

Detour	Diversion
Divided highway	Dual carriageway
No passing	No overtaking
Railroad crossing	Level crossing
Traffic circle	Roundabout
Yield	Give way

E

ELECTRIC CURRENT

The U.S. uses 110–115 volt, 60-cycle A.C. Plugs are small, flat, and two- or three-pronged; foreigners will need an adapter for shavers, etc.

EMBASSIES and CONSULATES

Few English-speaking countries maintain a consulate in Florida. The nearest are:

Australia:	630 Fifth Avenue, New York Tel. (212) 408-8400
Canada:	1251 Avenue of the Americas, New York Tel. (212) 596-1700
Eire:	515 Madison Avenue New York Tel. (212) 319-2555
New Zealand:	780 Third Avenue, New York Tel. (212) 832-4038
South Africa:	333 East 38th Street, New York Tel. (212) 213-4880
United Kingdom:	245 Peachtree Center Avenue. NE, Atlanta, Georgia Tel. (404) 524-5856

(The office in Miami is for trade matters only: Suite 2110 Brickell Bay Tower, 1001 S. Bayshore Drive, Miami; tel. (305) 374 1522.)

EMERGENCIES *(See also* MEDICAL CARE *and* POLICE.*)*

Dial 911, and the operator will ask if you want police, ambulance, or the fire department.

All towns and cities have a 24-hour number to call in case of emergency, if you need a doctor or a dentist. For a doctor in the Miami area, phone 324-8717. For a dentist the number is 667-3647.

ETIQUETTE

Many Americans are very polite, saying "Sir" and "Ma'am" to strangers and service staff. Oddly enough, though, requests often consist of "Gimme" and "I need," unaccompanied by "please." "Thank you" always receives a response such as "You're welcome" (or "You're quite welcome," "quite" meaning "very").

G

GETTING TO FLORIDA

Because fares and conditions change frequently, it is advisable to consult travel agents for the latest information.

FROM NORTH AMERICA

By Air: Miami, Fort Lauderdale, West Palm Beach, Orlando (the airport closest to Walt Disney World), Tampa, St. Petersburg, and Sarasota are easily accessible from the larger U.S. cities, with many non-stop flights daily to major centres.

By Bus: Florida destinations are linked to all major centres by Greyhound, which has merged with its previous main rival, Trailways.

By Rail: Amtrak advertises a variety of bargain fares, including Excursion and Family fares and tour packages with hotel and guide included. It runs a car-carrying train between Lorton near Washington D.C. and Sanford near Orlando.

By Car: Travellers coming down the east coast can take I-95 via Washington and Savannah. The shortest route from the west is I-10, passing Tucson, El Paso, Houston, and Mobile.

FROM THE U.K.

By Air: There are several daily non-stop flights from Heathrow and Gatwick to Miami, as well as other non-stops to Orlando.

FROM OTHER EUROPEAN CITIES

Non-stop flights operate from Frankfurt to Orlando and Miami, from Amsterdam to Orlando, and from Paris, Madrid, Helsinki, Shannon, Düsseldorf, Cologne, Munich, Rome, and Milan to Miami. There are many one-stop flights from other points.

Fares available include first class, economy, Excursion, APEX (Advance Purchase Excursion), Super-APEX and special "ticket sales" available through travel agents. In general, the longer ahead you book, the lower the fare, with the exception of stand-by fares which apply only at certain times of year. Some U.S. airlines offer travellers from abroad a discount on the cost of internal flights, or flat-rate, unlimited-travel tickets for specific periods.

Charter flights and package tours. Most charter flights must be booked and paid for well in advance. Many package tours are available: camper holidays, coach tours, excursions to Walt Disney World, or the Bahamas, trips to other American cities and sights, etc. Most Caribbean cruises originate in Florida ports.

Some two-centre holidays divide their time between Orlando and one of the beaches (east or west coast). Other combinations offer Orlando plus a short cruise or a spell on a Caribbean island.

Baggage. You may check in, free, two suitcases of normal size. One piece of hand luggage which fits under the aircraft seat may also be carried on board. Confirm size and weight restrictions with your travel agent or airline when booking your ticket.

It is advisable to insure all luggage for the duration of your trip, preferably as part of a general travel insurance policy. Any travel agent can arrange this.

GUIDES and TOURS

Some of the larger attractions provide the services of a guide. At Walt Disney World's Magic Kingdom, for example, ask at the Town Hall. Foreign-language guides are on call to take visitors on a quick tour, including a selection of rides.

Florida

Sightseeing tours by bus or "tram" are available in most cities and resorts. One-day bus tours from Miami to Disney World are not recommended — they don't allow enough time once you get there.

Pleasure cruises operate from many resorts, touring the coast, the inlets, lakes, rivers, and swamps, some serving meals on board or stopping at a restaurant. Miami and Miami Beach are well served, with tours and cruises of up and down the coast. At Key Largo you can take a glass-bottomed boat to view the coral reefs. Tours and cruises are also available in Fort Lauderdale, West Palm Beach, St. Petersburg, Sarasota, Naples, Tarpon Springs, and Key West.

L

LANGUAGE

Miami is virtually a bilingual city, and such has been the influence of refugees, mainly from Cuba, that you'll hear as much Spanish as English. Most English-speaking foreigners are familiar with American words and phrases. However, here are a few which can cause confusion.

US	British	US	British
admission	**entry fee**	minister	**vicar**
bathroom	**toilet**	no admission	**free entry**
bill	**note (money)**	purse	**handbag**
billfold	**wallet**	rest room	**toilet**
check	**bill (restaurant)**	round-trip ticket	**return ticket**
collect call	**reverse charges**	second floor	**first floor**
elevator	**lift**	sidewalk	**pavement**
first floor	**ground floor**	stand in line	**queue up**
gas	**petrol**	trailer	**caravan**
liquor	**spirits**	underpass	**subway**
liquor store	**off-license**		

LAUNDRY and DRY-CLEANING

Most larger hotels offer these services, at a price. Some hotels have coin-operated washing machines and dryers.

LOST PROPERTY

Air, rail, and bus terminals and many stores have special "lost and found" areas. Restaurants put aside lost articles in the hope that someone will claim them. If your lost property is valuable contact the police. If you lose your passport, get in touch with your consulate immediately.

M

MAPS

Welcome stations on main highways and ports of entry hand out free maps, and the local chamber of commerce or tourist authority will give or sell you maps with attractions marked on them. Service stations dispense maps from vending machines, and quite good maps are given out when you hire a car. The maps in this book were prepared by Falk-Verlag.

MEDICAL CARE *(See also* EMERGENCIES.*)*

Foreigners should note the U.S. doesn't provide free medical services, and that treatment is expensive. Arrangements should therefore be made in advance for temporary health insurance (through a travel agent or an insurance company).

"Health-First" clinics offer less prohibitively expensive treatment than private practitioners. Emergency rooms of hospitals will treat anyone in need of speedy attention, including hospitalization in a community ward. If you arrive in Florida after flying through several time zones, take it easy the first couple of days. Doctors recommend that visitors eat lightly initially, and get plenty of rest.

Beware of the powerful sun. Start with a high protection factor (20 or more) sunscreen or sunblock, and build up a tan gradually in small doses. Drink plenty of water. It is all too easy to become dehydrated — the warning signs are headaches and lassitude.

Visitors from the U.K. will find that some medicines sold over the counter at home can only be bought on prescription in the U.S. There's no shortage of drugstores, or pharmacies; a few of them stay open late at night.

MONEY MATTERS

Currency. The dollar is divided into 100 cents.

Banknotes: $1, $2 (rare), $5, $10, $20, $50, and $100. Larger denominations are not in general circulation. All notes except the new $100 bills, are the same size and colour, so beware of mixing them up.

Coins: 1¢ (called a "penny"), 5¢ ("nickel"), 10¢ ("dime"), 25¢ ("quarter"), 50¢ ("half dollar"), and $1. Only the first four are commonly used. You may inadvertently be given Canadian or other foreign coins in your change. Canadian coins are worth about 15% less than U.S. ones, and they do not work in automatic machines such as telephones.

Banks and currency exchange. Banking hours are usually from 9 a.m. to 2 or 3 p.m., Monday to Friday, but take note that very few banks change foreign currency. Walt Disney World's banks are a notable exception. Even in major cities, there may be only one counter in one bank able to handle foreign money. American hotel receptionists are distrustful of foreign banknotes, and they may offer a low exchange rate (so be aware of the exact rate before changing money). It is simpler to carry U.S. dollar traveller's cheques, major credit cards, and some cash in dollars.

When changing money or traveller's cheques, ask for $20 notes, which are accepted everywhere, as some establishments will refuse larger notes unless they nearly equal the amount to be paid. In fact $100 notes seem to circulate more outside the U.S. than inside, fakes included.

Credit cards. When shopping or paying hotel bills, you may be asked: "Cash or charge?," meaning you have the choice of paying in cash or by credit card. Businesses are wary of little-known cards, but most accept the top American or international cards. You'll often need some form of identification when charging your purchase.

Many service stations and other businesses will not take money at night, only cards. Outside normal office hours, it's sometimes impossible to rent cars and pay bills with cash.

Traveller's cheques. These are safer than cash. They can quickly be exchanged as long as they are in U.S. dollars. Banks will usually want to see your passport or other form of identity document ("ID"), but many hotels, shops, and restaurants will accept them directly in lieu of cash, especially those issued by American banks. Change only small amounts at a time: keep the balance of your cheques in your hotel safe if possible and make a note of serial numbers, and where and when you used each cheque.

Prices. Most displayed prices do not include a state sales tax of 6.5% — it's added when you pay. The same applies to your hotel bill, which may be further increased by local taxes.

Prices vary considerably in the U.S. For moderately priced goods, visit the big department or discount stores. Small independent grocery stores, drugstores and 24-hour "convenience stores" have price mark-ups of 10–70% over the supermarkets, but independent service stations are cheaper than those of the large oil companies.

PLANNING YOUR BUDGET

To give you an idea of what to expect, here's a list of average prices. However, they must be taken as broad guidelines, as inflation gradually pushes prices upwards.

Airport transfer. Taxi from Miami International Airport to downtown Miami $22; to Miami Beach up to $27. Super Shuttle $10–20, depending on destination.

Taxi from Orlando International Airport to International Drive $25, shuttle $15; to Walt Disney World $38, shuttle $12–15.

Baby-sitters. $4–5 per hour for one or two children, plus transport expenses. Hotels charge $6–8 per hour.

Florida

Bicycle hire. $3 per hour; $5–15 per day; $20–35 per week.

Campground. $8–35 per day, per site (i.e. space).

Car hire. Prices vary widely with the company and the season, and depend on what insurance is included (see page 105). A typical price for a mid-size car with unlimited mileage, fully insured, high season might be $36 per day, $169 per week.

Cigarettes. Pack of 20: American $2, foreign brands higher.

Diving. Half-day from boat with equipment $57; diving school $100/day.

Entertainment. Cinema $4–8.50; nightclub/discotheque $5–20 cover charge, $4–6 drinks; dinner show $30–75.

Golf. $25–80 (including cart).

Hairdressers. Man's haircut $7–25; Woman's haircut $10–25; cut, shampoo and set $17–50; colouring $20–60.

Hotels. Double room with bath: deluxe $120 and up; medium price $80–120; budget $40–60. Motels $40–75. There are big seasonal variations.

Laundry. Shirt $1.50; blouse $3.75.

Dry-cleaning. Jacket $4.50 and up; trousers $2.50 and up; dress $6 and up.

Meals and drinks. Continental breakfast $4–6; full breakfast $6–10; lunch in snack bar $5–10; in restaurant $8–14; dinner $15–30 (more with entertainment); fast-food meal $3–5; coffee $1; beer $2.50–3.50; glass of wine $3–5; carafe $6–10; bottle $10–20; cocktail $4–6.

Museums. $4–10.

Petrol (gasoline). $1.10 per U.S. gallon (approx. 4 litres).

Swamp airboat rides. $5–8 (45 minutes); glass-bottom boat $14.

Taxis. Meters start at $1.25, then $1.75 per mile in Miami.

Theme parks. Busch Gardens $34.95; Kennedy Space Center free, bus tours $7; IMAX film $4; Parrot Jungle $10.50; Sea World $39.95; Wet 'n' Wild $24.95; Universal Studios $38.50.

Walt Disney World: one-day ticket (Magic Kingdom or Disney-MGM Studios or EPCOT Center) adult $38.50, child 3–9 $31; four-day Super Pass (all parks) adult $132, child $103.50; five-day World-Hopper Pass (all parks and other facilities) adult $196, child $157.

NEWSPAPERS and MAGAZINES

Local newspapers and the national daily *U.S.A. Today* are sold in drugstores and from vending machines. Special newsstands carry the *New York Times* and the *Wall Street Journal,* as well as a variety of other newspapers. Two daily papers are printed in Miami: the *Miami Herald (El Nuovo Miami Herald* in Spanish) and the *Diario Las Américas.* The *Orlando Sentinel* provides information about Central Florida. A local paper will put you in touch with community news and list TV programmes, opening hours of attractions, grocery-store bargains, etc.

Most Florida cities have their own magazines with articles on events. Look for free "What's On" type magazines in hotels (for example *Welcome to Miami and the Beaches*).

OPENING HOURS

Most shops and businesses are open from 8 or 9 a.m. (larger stores from 9:30 or 10 a.m.) to 5 or 6 p.m. Some stores and chain-restaurants never close. Small restaurants usually open at 6 a.m. and close by 11 p.m.

The following are the opening hours of some of the sites mentioned in this guide. However, it's worth telephoning ahead of time to check. In many cases, hours are extended during holiday periods.

Florida

Miami

Ancient Spanish Monastery.
    Monday–Saturday 10 a.m.–4 p.m.
    Sunday 12 noon–4:30 p.m.

Bass Museum of Art.
    Tuesday–Saturday 10 a.m.–5 p.m.
    Sunday 1–5 p.m.
    1–9 p.m. second and fourth Wednesday of each month.

Fairchild Tropical Garden.
    Daily 9:30 a.m.–4:30 p.m.

Lowe Art Museum.
    Tuesday–Saturday 10 a.m.–5 p.m.
    Sunday 1–5 p.m.

Metro-Dade Cultural Center.
    Monday–Tuesday 10 a.m.–5 p.m.
    (except Thursdays 10 a.m.–9 p.m.)
    Sunday 12 noon–5 p.m.

Metrozoo. Daily 9:30 a.m.–5:30 p.m., box office closes at 4 p.m.

Monkey Jungle. Daily 9:30 a.m.–5 p.m.

Museum of Science and Planetarium. Daily 10 a.m.–6 p.m.

Parrot Jungle. Daily 9:30 a.m.–6 p.m.

Seaquarium. Daily 9:30 a.m.–6.00 p.m.
    Box office closes at 4:30 p.m.

Vizcaya. Daily 9.30 a.m.–4:30 p.m. Closed Christmas Day.

Fort Lauderdale

Ocean World. Daily 10 a.m.–6 p.m. Box office closes at 4:30 p.m.

Fort Myers

Edison Winter Home. Monday–Saturday 9 a.m.–3:30 p.m.
    Sunday 12:30 a.m.–3:30 p.m. Closed Thanksgiving
    (fourth Thursday in November) and Christmas Day.

Kennedy Space Center
    Daily 9 a.m.–dusk. Last bus tour 4.30 p.m.
    Closed Christmas Day.

Key West

Ernest Hemingway House. Daily 9 a.m.–5 p.m.

Key West Lighthouse. Daily 9:30 a.m.–5 p.m.

Truman Little White House. Daily 9 a.m.–5 p.m.

Orlando

Sea World. Daily 9 a.m.–7 p.m. Extended hours seasonally.

Universal Studios. 9 a.m.–11 p.m. Times vary seasonally.

Walt Disney World. Ride and attractions open daily from 9 a.m.
but it's worth arriving by 8.30 a.m. Closing times vary
from park to park and season to season, from 7 p.m. to 11 p.m.

Wet 'n' Wild. Daily 10 a.m.–5 p.m. in spring and autumn
9 a.m.–10 or 11 p.m. in summer. Hours vary by season.

Palm Beach/West Palm Beach

Flagler Museum. Tuesday–Saturday 10 a.m.–5 p.m.
Sunday 12 noon–5 p.m.

Lion Country Safari. Daily 9:30 a.m.–5:30 p.m.
Gate closes at 4:30 p.m.

Norton Gallery of Art. Tuesday–Saturday 10 a.m.–5 p.m.
Sunday 1–5 p.m.

St. Augustine

Castillo de San Marcos. Daily 8:45 a.m.–4:45 p.m.
Closed Christmas Day.

St. Petersburg

Museum of Fine Arts. Tuesday–Saturday 10 a.m.–5 p.m.
Sunday 1–5 p.m. Third Thursday of the month open until 9 p.m.

Salvador Dali Museum. Tuesday–Saturday 9:30 a.m.–5:30 p.m.
Sunday 1–5 p.m.

Sarasota

Bellm's Cars and Music of Yesterday. Daily 9:30 a.m.–5:30 p.m.

Ringling Museum Complex. Daily 10 a.m.–5.30 p.m.

Florida

Tampa

Busch Gardens. Daily 9:30 a.m.–6 p.m.
Extended hours during holidays, summer.

Winter Haven

Cypress Gardens. Daily 9:30 a.m.–5:30 p.m.
(occasionally extended hours).

P

PHOTOGRAPHY and VIDEO

Camera shops sell film, but drugstores and supermarkets supply the same at discount prices. Wait until you are home to develop transparency film because it may take longer than you think. Do not store film in the car: it may get so hot that film will be damaged.

Airport security X-ray machines are safe for normal film, whether exposed or unused. Super-fast film may be affected and you should ask for separate inspection.

Videotape is available for all types of cameras. Note that pre-recorded tapes bought in the U.S. may not function on European systems (and vice versa) unless the equipment has special features. The same applies to the video cameras you can rent at some attractions. Tapes can be converted, but only at considerable expense.

POLICE

City police are concerned with local crime and traffic violations, while Highway Patrol officers (also called State Troopers) ensure highway safety, and are on the lookout for people speeding or driving under the influence of alcohol or drugs.. For emergencies, dial 911 (fire, police, ambulance).

POST OFFICES

The U.S. postal service deals only with mail; telephone and telegraph services are operated by other companies. Post letters in the blue curbside boxes. You can buy stamps from machines in post office entrance halls after hours. Stamps from machines in hotels and shops cost a lot more than face value.

Post office hours are from 8 a.m. to 5 p.m., Monday to Friday, from 8 a.m. to 12 noon on Saturdays. In larger towns, one branch usually remains open later in the evening, until 9 p.m. or so.

Poste restante (general delivery). You can have mail marked "General Delivery" sent to you care of the main post office of any town. The letters will be held for no more than a month. Take your driving license or passport with you for identification.

PUBLIC HOLIDAYS

If a holiday, such as Christmas Day, falls on a Sunday, banks and most stores close on the following day. At long weekends (such as the one following Thanksgiving), offices are closed for four days. Many restaurants never shut, however, even at Christmas.

New Years Day	**1 January**
Martin Luther King Day	**Third Monday in January**
Washington's Birthday	**Third Monday in February**
Memorial Day	**Last Monday in May**
Independence Day	**4 July**
Labor Day	**First Monday in September**
Columbus Day	**Second Monday in October**
Veterans' Day	**11 November**
Thanksgiving Day	**Fourth Thursday in November**
Christmas Day	**25 December**

R

RADIO and TV

Numerous AM and FM radio stations broadcast pop, rock, and Country and Western music; most large cities also have a classical station.

Almost every hotel room has a television carrying many channels, some 24 hours a day. Local news begins around 6 p.m., with national and international news from New York at 6:30 or 7 p.m. CNN transmits news around the clock.

RELIGION

Saturday newspapers often list the church services of the following day, with details of visiting preachers. Besides Catholic, Episcopalian, Presbyterian, and Methodist churches there are many fundamentalist and Southern Baptist denominations. In Miami Beach and along the Gold Coast there are numerous synagogues, and there's at least one in every main town.

S

SMOKING

Smoking is banned in many public buildings and places of entertainment, including the attractions, rides, and waiting areas in theme parks. Most restaurants have smoking and non-smoking areas: you will be asked which you want. Some restaurants do not allow smoking at all. Many hotels have non-smoking rooms.

T

TELEPHONES

American telephone companies are efficient and reliable. Dialling directions are always posted beside public telephones.

Local calls. Lift the receiver, deposit 25¢ in the slot, wait for the dial tone, then dial the seven-digit number. The operator will automatically inform you of any additional charge, so have some change ready. For local directory inquiries, dial 411. For local operator assistance, and for help within the same area code, dial 0.

Long-distance calls may be dialled direct from a pay phone if you follow the posted directions. The prefix 1- usually has to be dialled before the number. If you don't know the correct area code, dial 0 for operator assistance. Long-distance calls cost more from a pay phone than from a private one. International direct dial calls require the prefix 011, then the country code.

Telephone rates are listed in the introduction to the white pages of the telephone directory, along with information on personal (person-to-person), reverse-charge (collect), and credit-card calls. Some telephone companies no longer accept the major credit cards. All numbers with an 800 prefix are toll-free.

Fax. You can send faxes from many hotels, and from office-service bureaux found in some shopping malls.

Telegrams. American telegraph companies offer domestic and overseas services, as well as telex facilities, and are listed in the *Yellow Pages*. You can telephone the telegraph office, dictate the message, and have the charge added to your hotel bill, or dictate it from a coin-operated phone and pay on the spot. A letter telegram (night letter) costs about half the rate of a normal telegram. Note that the U.K. does not have a telegram service: your message will just be delivered with the mail.

TIME DIFFERENCES

The continental U.S. has four time zones; Florida (like New York City) is on Eastern Standard Time. Between April and October, Daylight Saving Time is adopted and clocks move ahead one hour. The following chart shows the time in various cities in winter when it's noon in Florida:

Los Angeles	**Miami**	London	Sydney
9 a.m.	**noon**	5 p.m.	4 a.m.
Sunday	**Sunday**	Sunday	Monday

TIPPING

Waiters and waitresses earn most of their salary from tips; often they are paid little else. In simple eating houses you usually pay the cashier on your way out, after leaving a tip on the table. Otherwise, you can write in the tip on a credit card slip: they always leave a space for it. Cinema or theatre ushers and filling-station attendants are not tipped.

Florida

Some suggestions:

Guide	10–15%
Hairdresser/barber	15%
Hotel porter (per bag)	50¢–$1 (minimum $1)
Taxi driver	15%
Waiter	15–20%
	(unless service has been added)

TOILETS

You can find toilets in restaurants, railway stations, and large stores, as well as hotels and restaurants. In some places you must deposit a coin, in others you can leave a tip for the attendant if there is one.

Americans use the terms "restroom," "powder room," "bathroom," (private) and "ladies" or "men's room" to indicate the toilet.

TOURIST INFORMATION OFFICES

For information before your trip, write to:

United States Travel & Tourism Administration
PO Box 1EN, London W1A 1EN
Tel. 071-495 4466, fax 071-495 4377

Florida Division of Tourism in Europe
1st floor, 18–24 Westbourne Grove
London W2 5RH
Tel. 071-243-8519

State of Florida Division of Tourism, Visitor Inquiries
126 W. Van Buren Street, Tallahassee, FL 32399-2000
Tel. (888) 735-2872

Information is also freely dispensed from welcome stations at the main entry points to the state and in hotels, but the chief source of tourist information in any town is the local chamber of commerce.

TRANSPORT. *(See also* AIRPORTS, GETTING TO FLORIDA, CAR HIRE, *and* DRIVING.)

Buses. *(See also* GUIDES AND TOURS.) The largest company, Greyhound Lines, merged with its rival Trailways, serves all major resorts and attractions. As well as the Florida network, it offers services to and from cities all over the U.S. (New York to Orlando takes around 25 hours.) Smaller bus lines provide local shuttle services between hotels and attractions, as well as sightseeing tours. Visitors can buy unlimited rover passes (these can only be bought outside the U.S.), valid for a specified length of time, to go anywhere in the country by Greyhound bus at a flat rate.

City buses. Rule number one: have the exact change ready to deposit in the box beside the driver. Miami buses can be crowded and frantic, but, generally speaking, service is regular and punctual.

Miami Metrorail. Miami has an elevated railway running north-south through the centre of the city. The air-conditioned trains operate at frequent intervals from 5:30 a.m. to midnight.

Taxis. Taxis always carry a roof sign and can easily be recognized. Most have meters, and the rates are generally marked on the doors. Some cruise the streets, especially in city centres. To phone for a taxi, look in the *Yellow Pages* under "Taxicabs." Tip 15% of the fare.

Trains. Amtrak (National Railroad Passenger Corporation) offers a variety of bargain fares, including Excursion and Family fares; the USA Railpass can only be purchased abroad, but many package tours are available in the U.S. Air-conditioned trains link Florida's main towns with urban centres throughout the U.S. (New York to Orlando takes 24 hours.) The Tri-Rail system connects Miami and the international airport with Gold Coast cities and resorts.

TRAVELLERS with DISABILITIES

More efforts have been made in the United States than almost any other country to enable those with disabilities to get around. Hotels and public buildings have wheelchair entrances and special toilets.Theme parks make as many of their attractions as possible accessible to wheelchairs, and some provide special help to sight - and hearing - impaired visitors.

WEIGHTS and MEASURES

The United States is one of the few countries that have not yet adopted the metric system, and has no plans to do so at present.

Florida

Length

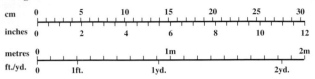

Weight

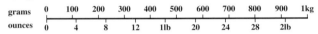

Temperature

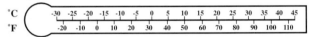

Fluid measures

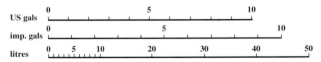

Y

YOUTH HOSTELS

There are only about 160 hostels in the US. Most are outside the big cities, and the distances between them can be enormous. Some budget hotels offer a large discount to International YHA (Youth Hostel Association) members. There is no age limit. For further information, apply to: American Youth Hostel Association, Inc., National Campus, Delaplane, VA 22025.

Recommended Hotels

Long-established and still growing as a holiday destination, Florida offers a huge choice of accommodations. All resorts have representatives of the big chains and franchises, as well as rows of budget motels. The Orlando area, including Walt Disney World, has more hotel rooms than any city in the United States. Competition in the highly developed hospitality industry means that you'll be assured of value for money, whether you choose the most luxurious resort, a modest motel, or something in between. Here we can only make a small selection. We have subdivided the list by area, following the same order as the Where to Go section of this guide. Each entry is marked with a symbol indicating the price range, per night, for a double room with bath, excluding breakfast. Sales tax of 6½% is added to hotel bills.

In the US, rates quoted are for the room, not per person. Additional occupants over two may be charged a small premium. A few places include a simple Continental breakfast. Always ask about special-rate packages, e.g, for stays of a few days, lower midweek rates, and off-season rates. (Two symbols, e.g, ✪✪/✪✪✪, indicate major seasonal variations between price ranges.)

✪	up to $80
✪✪	$80–$120
✪✪✪	$120–$220
✪✪✪✪	$220 and over

MIAMI BEACH TO AVENTURA

The Alexander ✪✪✪✪ *5225 Collins Avenue, Miami Beach, FL 33140; tel. (305) 865-6500, fax 864-8525.* All-suite luxury in pink tower near its own wide beach. Landscaped gardens and pools. 211 rooms.

Colony ✪✪ *736 Ocean Drive, Miami Beach, FL 33139; tel. (305) 673-0088 or (800) 223-6725, fax 534-7409.* Art-Deco treasure, restored and now a focus of fashionable South Beach. 36 rooms.

Doral Ocean Beach Resort ✪✪✪ *4833 Collins Avenue, Miami Beach, FL 33140; tel. (305) 532-3600, fax 532-2334.* Tower on the ocean. Comprehensive fitness facilities, tennis, pool, boating, golf nearby. 420 rooms.

Fontainebleau Hilton ✪✪✪/✪✪✪✪ *4441 Collins Avenue, Miami Beach, FL 33140; tel. (305) 538-2000 or (800) 548-8886, fax 531-9274.* Huge white curving blocks in lush grounds next to the beach. Pools, tennis. 1206 rooms.

Sheraton Bal Harbour Beach Resort ✪✪✪/✪✪✪✪ *9701 Collins Avenue, Bal Harbour, FL 33154; tel. (305) 865-7511 or (800) 325-3535, fax 864-2601.* Landscaped resort on the ocean. Tennis, pools, golf. 650 rooms.

Turnberry Isle Yacht & Country Club ✪✪✪✪ *19999 W. Country Club Drive, Aventura, FL 33180; tel. (305) 932-6200 or (800) 327-7028, fax 933-6560.* Elegant resort with ocean club, pools, golf courses. 357 rooms.

MIAMI AND AREA

Biscayne Bay Marriott ✪✪/✪✪✪ *1633 N. Bayshore Drive, Miami, FL 33132; tel. (305) 374-3900 or (800) 228-9290, fax 375-0597.* Downtown bayfront hotel adjoining shopping mall. Pool. 584 rooms.

Doubletree ✪✪ *2649 S. Bayshore Drive, Coconut Grove, FL 33133; tel. (305) 858-2500 or (800) 872-7749, fax 858-5776.* Spacious rooms with views of the bay and the "Grove." Pool, tennis. 190 rooms.

Grand Bay ✪✪✪✪ *2669 S. Bayshore Drive, Coconut Grove, FL 33133; tel. (305) 858-9600 or (800) 327-2788, fax 859-2026.* Spacious luxury overlooking Biscayne Bay. Pool. 181 rooms.

Mayfair House ✪✪✪/✪✪✪✪ *3000 Florida Avenue, Coconut Grove, FL 33133; tel. (305) 441-0000 or (800) 433-4555, fax 447-9173.* All-suite hotel in the heart of the "Grove." Pool. 181 rooms.

Miami Airport Inn ✪✪ *1550 NW Lejeune Road, Miami, FL 33126; tel. (305) 871-2345, fax 871-2811.* Reasonable economy near international airport. Pool. 209 rooms.

Sonesta Beach Hotel and Tennis Club ✪✪✪✪ *350 Ocean Drive, Key Biscayne, FL 33149; tel. (305) 361-2021 or (800) 766-3782, fax 365-2096.* Family-orientated resort on the ocean. Tennis, pools, golf course adjoining. 300 rooms.

THE GOLD COAST

Radisson Bahia Mar Beach Resort ✪✪/✪✪✪ *801 Seabreeze Boulevard, Fort Lauderdale, Florida, FL 33316; tel. (305) 764-2233 or (800) 333-3333, fax 523-5424.* On the sea, with vast yacht and fishing marina adjoining. Tennis, pools, watersports. 300 rooms.

The Breakers ✪✪✪/✪✪✪✪ *1 S. Country Road, Palm Beach, FL 33480; tel. (561) 655-6611 or (800) 533-3141, fax 659-8403.* Massive oceanfront palace dating from the 1920s, dominates the middle of Palm Beach. Two golf courses, tennis, croquet, pools. 528 rooms.

Days Inn ✪/✪✪ *1700 W. Broward Boulevard, Fort Lauderdale, Florida, FL 33312; tel. (954) 463-2500 or (800) 866-650, fax 763-6504.* Economy in downtown Fort Lauderdale. Pool. 144 rooms.

Marriott Harbor Beach Resort ✪✪✪/✪✪✪✪ *3030 Holiday Drive, Fort Lauderdale, FL 33316; tel. (954) 525-4000 or (800) 228-6543, fax 766-6165.* Resort on Atlantic Ocean. Pools, tennis, watersports. 625 rooms.

Ocean Grand ✪✪✪/✪✪✪✪ *2800 S. Ocean Boulevard, Palm Beach, FL 33480; tel. (561) 582-2800, fax 547-1557.* Newer luxury resort of low-rise buildings near the sea. Pools and gardens. 213 rooms.

Bonaventure Resort and Spa ✪✪✪/✪✪✪✪ *250 Racquet Club Road, Fort Lauderdale, Florida, FL 33326; tel. (954) 389-*

3300 or (800) 327-809, fax 384-0563. Extensive resort some way inland. Golf, tennis, squash, health spa, pools. 500 rooms.

THE SPACE COAST AND ST. AUGUSTINE

Daytona Beach Hilton ✪✪/✪✪✪ *2637 S. Atlantic Avenue, Daytona Beach, FL 32118; tel. (904) 767-7350, fax 760-3651.* At the quieter end of the beach. Pool, tennis. 215 rooms.

Best Western Ocean Inn ✪ *5500 N. Atlantic Avenue, Cocoa Beach, FL 32931; tel. (407) 784-2550, fax 868-7124.* Budget hotel near beach. Pool. 100 rooms.

Perry's Ocean Edge Resort ✪✪ *2209 S. Atlantic Avenue, Daytona Beach, FL 32118; tel. (904) 255-0581 or (800) 447-0002, fax 258-7315.* Beach-front hotel. Pools, watersports. 204 rooms.

Ponce de León Resort ✪✪✪ *4000 U.S. Hwy 1 North, St. Augustine, FL 32085; tel. (904) 824-2821 or (800) 228-2821, fax 824-8254.* Country-club setting with golf, tennis, and pools. Near beach. 204 rooms.

Wakulla Motel ✪✪ *3550 N. Atlantic Avenue Cocoa Beach, FL 32931; tel. (407) 783-2230 or (800) 992-5852, fax 783-0980.* Suite motel; each room has its own kitchen. Pools, gardens. Close to beach. 116 rooms.

WITHIN WALT DISNEY WORLD

Guests in Disney-owned accommodations have privileges in making reservations for shows, dinner, etc. Car parking at the theme parks is free for them, and entry to the parks by Disney transportation is guaranteed. These advantages can offset the somewhat higher prices of rooms within Disney World. The central hotel number for Disney properties is (407) W-DISNEY.

Caribbean Beach Resort ✪✪ *Walt Disney World, Lake Buena Vista, FL 32830-0100; tel. (407) 934-3400, fax 354-1866.* Near EPCOT. Colourful "village" design around a lake with themed pool and marina. 2,112 rooms.

Contemporary Resort ✪✪✪✪ *Walt Disney World, Lake Buena Vista, FL 32830-0100; tel. (407) 824-1000, fax 354-1865.* 15-storey "vaulting horse" shape, next to Magic Kingdom. Pools, marina. 1,041 rooms, 80 suites.

Dixie Landings Resort ✪✪ *Walt Disney World, Lake Buena Vista, FL 32830-0100; tel. (407) 934-6000, fax 934-5777.* Not far from EPCOT; convenient for all areas of WDW. Pools, waterway. 2,048 rooms.

Grand Floridian Beach Resort ✪✪✪✪ *Walt Disney World, Lake Buena Vista, FL 32830; tel. (407) 824-3000, fax 354-1866.* Recreation of Victorian splendour. Monorail to Magic Kingdom. Pools, marina, beach. 901 rooms.

Walt Disney World Dolphin ✪✪✪✪ *Operated by Sheraton, PO Box 22653, Lake Buena Vista, FL 32830-2653; tel. (407) 934-4000 or (800) 227-1500, fax 934-4884.* Near EPCOT International Gateway. Vast triangular landmark tower. Marina, pools. 1,509 rooms.

Walt Disney World Swan ✪✪✪✪ *Operated by Westin, PO Box 22786, Lake Buena Vista, FL 32830; tel. (407) 934-3000 or (800) 248-7926, fax 934-4499.* A short walk to EPCOT International Gateway. Arc-roof tower topped by swans. Marina, pools, beach. 758 rooms.

Wilderness Lodge ✪✪✪ *Walt Disney World, Lake Buena Vista, FL 32830; tel. (407) 934-7639, fax 824-3232.* five-storey atrium supported by lodge-pole pines; replica geyser erupts hourly. Pool. 728 rooms

Yacht Club Beach Club Resorts ✪✪✪ *Walt Disney World, Lake Buena Vista, FL 32830; tel. (407) 934-7000, fax 354-1866.* Twin recreations of 19th-century Massachusetts coast resort. Marina, pools, beach. 1,214 rooms.

DISNEY VILLAGE PLAZA HOTELS

Designated "Hotels of Walt Disney World," these are inside WDW but not Disney-owned.

Buena Vista Palace ✪✪✪ *1900 Buena Vista Drive, Lake Buena Vista, FL 32830; tel. (407) 827-2727 or (800) 327-2990, fax 827-6034.* Lakeside tower complex. Tennis, pools, gardens. 841 rooms.

Grosvenor Resort ✪✪✪ *1850 Hotel Plaza Boulevard, Lake Buena Vista, FL 32830; tel. (407) 828-4444 or (800) 624-4109, fax 828-8129.* Tower block with convention facilities. Tennis, pools. 630 rooms.

Hilton ✪✪✪ *1751 Hotel Plaza Boulevard, Lake Buena Vista, FL 32830; tel. (407) 827-4000, fax 827-6380.* C-shaped luxury block with restaurant, pools, tennis, 813 rooms.

The Courtyard by Marriott ✪✪✪ *1805 Hotel Plaza Boulevard, Lake Buena Vista, FL 32830; tel. (407) 828-8888 or (800) 223-9930, fax 827-4623.* fourteen-storey tower and lower annexe. Pools, garden, family-oriented dining. 323 rooms.

ORLANDO AND AREA

Days Inn Maingate West ✪✪ *5820 W. Irlo Bronson Memorial Hwy. (U.S. 192), Kissimmee, FL 34746; tel. (407) 396-1000, fax 396-1789.* Budget hotel. Pools. 604 rooms.

Delta Orlando ✪✪ *5715 Major Boulevard, Orlando, FL 32819; tel. (407) 351-3340, fax 351-5117.* Family-oriented budget resort. Pools, garden, tennis, mini-golf. 800 rooms.

Gateway Inn ✪✪ *7050 Kirkman Road, Orlando, FL 32819; tel. (407) 351-2000, fax 363-1835.* Family-orientated economy hotel. Pools. 354 rooms.

Harley Hotel ✪✪/✪✪✪ *151 E. Washington Street, Orlando, FL 32801; tel. (407) 841-3220, fax 849-1839.* Downtown lakeside hotel. Near Church Street entertainment. Pool. 305 rooms.

Holiday Inn Orlando North ✪✪ *626 Lee Road, Winter Park, FL 32810; tel. (407) 645-5600; fax 740-7912.* Four miles north of downtown Orlando. Pools. 202 rooms.

Hyatt Regency Grand Cypress Resort ✪✪/✪✪✪ *1 Grand Cypress Boulevard, Orlando, FL 32836; tel. (407) 239-1234 or (800) 233-1234, fax 239-3800.* Spacious resort and convention centre with extensive sports facilities including golf courses, tennis, pools, lake, sailing, equestrian centre, large gardens. 750 rooms.

Larson's Lodge Maingate ✪ *6075 W. Irlo Bronson Memorial Hwy. (US192), Kissimmee, FL 34747; tel. (407) 396-6100 or (800) 327-9074, fax 396-6965.* Budget hotel. Pools. 128 rooms.

Peabody Orlando ✪✪✪ *9801 International Drive, Orlando, FL 32819; tel. (407) 352-4000 or (800) 732-2639, fax 351-9177.* Towering 27-storey landmark with convention centre. Tennis, pool. 851 rooms.

Stouffer Renaissance Orlando Resort ✪✪✪ *6677 Sea Harbor Drive, Orlando, FL 32821; tel. (407) 351-5555 or (800) 327-6677, fax 351-9991.* Ten-storey tower and convention complex, suited to families. Pools, tennis, near Sea World. 778 rooms.

THE EVERGLADES

Flamingo Lodge Marina and Outpost Resort ✪✪ *Flamingo Lodge Highway, Flamingo, FL 33034; tel. (941) 695-3101 or (800) 650-3813, fax 695-3921.* Base for sailing, fishing, exploring the national park. 120 rooms.

THE FLORIDA KEYS

Cheeca Lodge ✪✪✪✪ *MM82, Overseas Hwy. Islamorada, Box 527, FL 33036; tel. (305) 664-4651 or (800) 327-2888, fax*

664-2893. Luxury seaside resort. Golf, tennis, pools, watersports. 203 rooms.

Pier House ✪✪✪ *1 Duval Street, Key West, FL 33040; tel. (305) 296-4600 or (800) 327-8340, fax 296-7569.* Next to Mallory Square and marina. Pool, small beach. 142 rooms.

Banyan Resort ✪✪✪ *323 Whitehead Street, Key West, FL 33040; tel. (305) 296-7786 or (800) 225-0639, fax 294-1107.* Luxury suites in a complex of restored Victorian homes. two pools, tropical gardens, close to town. 38 suites.

GULF COAST — NAPLES TO FORT MYERS

Admiral Lehigh Golf Resort ✪✪/✪✪✪ *225 E. Joel Boulevard, Lehigh, FL 33936; tel. (813) 369-2121, fax 368-1660.* Hotel situated in country club east of Fort Myers near I-75. Two 18-hole golf courses, floodlit tennis courts, pool. 121 rooms.

Edgewater Beach ✪✪/✪✪✪ *1901 Gulfshore Boulevard North, Naples, FL 33940; tel. (941) 262-6511 or (8))0 821-0916, fax 262-1243.* Quiet, elegant hotel with pool, facing directly onto the beach. 124 rooms.

Park Shore Resort ✪✪/✪✪✪ *600 Neapolitan Way, Naples, FL 33940; tel. (813) 263-2222 or (800) 548-2077, fax 263-0946.* All-suite complex of villas with full kitchen facilities. Pool, landscaped gardens. 156 rooms.

Registry Resort ✪✪✪/✪✪✪✪ *475 Seagate Drive, Naples, FL 33940; tel. (941) 597-3232 or (800) 247-9810, fax 597-3147.* Spacious and elegant resort with golf, tennis, fitness facilities, pools, beach. 474 rooms.

Sundial Beach & Tennis Resort ✪✪✪ *1451 Middle Gulf Drive, Sanibel Island, FL 33957; tel. (941) 472 4151 or (800) 237-4184, fax 472-1809.* Low-rise seafront resort with tennis courts and pools. 265 rooms.

Vanderbilt Inn ✪✪/✪✪✪ *11000 Gulf Shore Drive North, Naples, FL 33963; tel. (941) 597-3151, fax 597-3099.* Smaller seafront resort north of Naples. Pools. 148 rooms.

GULF COAST — TAMPA BAY AREA

Best Western Siesta Beach Resort ✪✪ *5311 Ocean Boulevard, Sarasota, FL 34242; tel. (813) 349-3211 or (800) 223-5786, fax 349-7915.* Budget resort on Siesta Key, close to "world's whitest sand." Beach, pool. 50 rooms.

Best Western Sirata Beach ✪✪/✪✪✪ *5390 Gulf Boulevard, St. Petersburg Beach, FL 33706; tel. (813) 367-2771 or (800) 344-5999, fax 360-6799.* Family-orientated resort facing the beach. Pools, sports. 155 rooms.

Holiday Inn Madeira Beach ✪✪ *15208 Gulf Boulevard, Madeira Beach, FL 33708; tel. (813) 392-2275 or (800) 465-4329, fax 393-4019.* On the white sandy beach north of St. Pete's. Pool, watersports, tennis. 147 rooms.

Hyatt Sarasota ✪✪✪ *1000 Boulevard of the Arts, Sarasota, FL 34236; tel. (941) 953-1234 or (800) 233-1234, fax 952-1987.* Near downtown, bay, and Van Wezel Hall. Pool, marina. 297 rooms.

Howard Johnson's Busch Gardens ✪ *4139 E. Busch Boulevard, Tampa, FL 33617; tel. (813) 988-9191, fax 988-9195.* Economy hotel close to Busch Gardens. Pool. 100 rooms.

Sheraton Grand ✪✪✪ *4860 W. Kennedy Boulevard, Tampa, FL 33609; tel. (813) 286-4400 or (800) 325-3535, fax 286-4053.* Close to international airport and Westshore business district. Large rooms, pool. 325 rooms.

Recommended Restaurants

Everywhere you turn, there's somewhere to eat, almost all open seven days a week. Here we give a selection of full-service restaurants, buffet restaurants, and food courts (multiple outlets sharing a table area). There is no space to list even a fraction of the vast number of restaurants and all-you-can-eat buffets well within our lowest price range. (See also the section on Eating Out in the main part of this guide, pages 94-98.)

Each entry is marked with a symbol indicating the price range, per person, for a dinner comprising starter or salad, main course, and dessert. (Drinks, gratuities, and 6½% sales tax are not included.)

✪	up to $15
✪✪	$15-30
✪✪✪	$30 and over

MIAMI AND MIAMI BEACH

Café Abbracci ✪✪✪ *318 Aragon Avenue, Coral Gables; tel. (305) 441-0700.* Northern Italian cuisine.

Islas Canarias ✪ *285 NW 27th Avenue, Miami; tel. (305) 649-0440.* Popular traditional Cuban cooking in Little Havana area. No credit cards.

Joe's Stone Crab ✪✪ *227 Biscayne Street, Miami Beach; tel. (305) 673-0365.* An institution since 1913, open from October to May.

Malaga ✪ *740 SW 8th Street, Miami; tel. (305) 858-4224.* Traditional Cuban and Spanish dishes on "Calle Ocho."

Los Ranchos ✪✪ *Bayside Marketplace, Miami; tel. (305) 375-0666*. Nicaraguan-style steakhouse.

Rascal House ✪ *17190 Collins Avenue, Miami Beach; tel. (305) 947-4581*. New York-style deli known for its hearty sandwiches and large portions.

Sakura ✪ *8225 SW 124th Street, Miami; tel. (305) 238-8462*. Sushi, tempura, teriyaki dishes.

WPA ✪✪ *685 Washington Avenue, Miami Beach; tel. (305) 534-1684*. Relaxed bistro-style modern American cooking with Italian and Tex-Mex variations.

Yuca ✪✪✪ *501 Lincoln Road, Miami Beach; tel. (305) 444-4448*. Upscale, advanced Cuban cuisine in an elegant setting.

THE GOLD COAST

Café Arugula ✪✪✪ *3110 N. Federal Highway, Lighthouse Point; tel. (305) 785-7732*. The best and brightest ingredients in New American cuisine.

Ruth's Chris Steak House ✪✪ *661 U.S. Highway 1, North Palm Beach; tel. (561) 863-0660*. Steaks and seafood specialities.

Studio One ✪✪ *2447 E. Sunrise Boulevard, Fort Lauderdale; tel. (954) 565-2052. Delicious* French- and Caribbean-influenced cuisine.

Testa's ✪✪ *221 Royal Poinciana Way, Palm Beach; tel. (561) 832-0992*. Established Italian and seafood eating place; with a garden courtyard.

TooJay's Gourmet Deli ✪ *313 Royal Poinciana Plaza, Poinciana Center, Palm Beach; tel. (561) 659-7232*. Generous sandwiches and delicatessen favourites in a relaxed atmosphere.

THE SPACE COAST AND ST. AUGUSTINE

The Shark House ✪ *2929 South A1A, Beverly Beach; tel. (904) 439-1000.* Bar-restaurant with fresh seafood and steaks, south of St. Augustine.

Live Oak Inn ✪✪ *448 South Beach Street, Daytona Beach; tel. (904) 252-4667.* American menu, elegant old house overlooking marina. Closed Mon.

The Pier Restaurant ✪✪ *Cocoa Beach Pier, 401 Meade Avenue, Cocoa Beach; tel. (407) 783-7549.* Elegant dining on the old wooden pier.

Raintree ✪✪✪ *102 San Marco Avenue, St. Augustine; tel. (904) 824-7211.* Superb international cuisine in elegant surroundings.

St. Regis ✪✪ *509 Seabreeze Boulevard, Daytona Beach; tel. (904) 252-8743.* An old home converted to inn and restaurant. Home cooking.

WALT DISNEY WORLD (including Village/Plaza)

Restaurant Akershus ✪✪ *Norway Pavilion, EPCOT.* Norwegian buffet of hot and cold dishes, from herring and salmon to goats' cheese and desserts. Call (407) WDW-DINE for reservations.

Biergarten Restaurant ✪✪ *Germany Pavilion, EPCOT.* Veal, smoked pork, bratwurst, and other German specialities. Call (407) WDW-DINE for reservations.

Bistro de Paris ✪✪✪ *France Pavilion, EPCOT.* Traditional French ambience. Colourful and inventive cuisine, the menu devised by master chefs. Call (407) WDW-DINE for reservations.